PARIS

MEMORIES OF TIMES PAST

75 PAINTINGS BY MORTIMER MENPES

WRITTEN BY SOLANGE HANDO
WITH COLIN INMAN, FLORENCE BESSON, AND ROBERTA FAULHABER-RAZAFY

A NOTE TO THE READER

In order to keep the pages of the book as uncluttered as possible,
all sources, notes and captions relating to illustrations other than
the main paintings have been grouped at the end of the book, and
will be found on pages 173–174.

The front endpaper is taken from *Paris-Atlas*,
published by Librairie Larousse, Paris, in 1906.
The back endpaper is taken from *Stielers Hand-Atlas*, published in Gotha in 1905.

First published in the UK in 2008 by Worth Press Ltd, Cambridge, United Kingdom

Florence Besson and Roberta Faulhaber-Razafy have asserted their rights under the
Copyright and Patents Act 1988 to be identified as the authors of the book

Copyright © 2008 Worth Press Ltd.
Concept, design and layout © 2008 Bookcraft Ltd.

All reasonable efforts have been made to trace original copyright holders

Project manager   John Button
Design manager   Lucy Guenot

Set in Centaur and Gill Sans by Bookcraft Ltd, Stroud, Gloucestershire
Printed in China by Imago

A Memories of Times Past title
www.memoriesoftimespast.com

ISBN 978 1 903025 67 3

CONTENTS

PARIS 1909

SOLANGE HANDO

In 1909, as today, the Eiffel Tower held her head high above Paris. Whether it had any future beyond that year, however, was doubtful. The twenty-year concession granted at the 1889 World Exhibition was about to expire, and an artist like Mortimer Menpes could not be sure that it would continue to be thought of as a timeless Paris landmark. He therefore chose not to include it in his artistic homage to the city he loved so much.

When it was constructed, the 1,063-foot-high Eiffel Tower was the world's tallest building, chosen unanimously out of 700 projects to mark the 1889 Exhibition. Yet even in its earliest days, artists and architects had protested against this "useless monster." Now that ownership of the site and structure was about to be returned to the city, the tower's opponents regained momentum, branding it ugly, outmoded, a "metal asparagus," a "gigantic smokestack" on the Parisian skyline.

enue des Champs Élysées. — LL.

1181 PARIS (XVe). Perspective du Champ-de-Mars et la Tour Eiffe

Previous page: A color photochrome of the Eiffel Tower, from *Paris*, published in 1910 by A. P. Etablissments Papeghin (top right); tinted image of the Eiffel Tower from *Encyclopedie du Siècle: Exposition de Paris 1900*, Montgredin et Cie (bottom); a 1908 postcard of the tower

The original competition stated clearly that the winning structure should be relatively simple to take down at the end of the concession, a state of affairs that suited its detractors.

But at the eleventh hour, the tower's defenders had a stroke of luck. Paris was about to witness the birth of a new wireless system, which needed a tall mast to direct radio waves across the city. What better location than the Eiffel Tower for a mast to service the new system? Without delay, an underground radio center was built below one of the pillars. The following year it would become an integral part of the International Time Service. Thus the "grand old lady" was saved, and Parisians and visitors alike continued to swoon at her feet.

In so many ways, the Paris of 1909 was a city worth swooning for. Only London and New York could rival her for world-class metropolitan status, but neither could touch her for romance and joie de vivre. It was a time for forgetting the past and welcoming the future.

The bitter defeat of the Franco-Prussian war, for more than thirty years, was now rarely mentioned; the degradingly racist Dreyfus Affair, which had distracted the country for years, had finally drawn to a close. After the social and political turmoil of the fin de siècle, the belle epoque was in full swing. In July 1909 the pacifist-socialist politician Aristide Briand, who in 1926 would share a Nobel Peace Prize with his German counterpart, Gustav Stresemann, was appointed prime minister. Rodin finally unveiled a marble monument to Victor Hugo, and the avant-garde Ballets Russes led by Diaghilev swept Paris off her feet. André Gide published his bestselling novel *Strait Is the Gate* (*La Porte Etroite*) and founded the literary magazine *Nouvelle Revue Française*, and Claude Debussy had recently composed the Children's Corner Suite, inspired by his daughter Chou-chou. The city held the first international air show. On the city's many cinema screens, the Pathé newsreel, first seen in Paris in 1900, was a regular source of news and entertainment, complementing the Parisian press, which printed millions of copies a day for every stratum of society.

Nearly a decade earlier, the start of the millennium had passed almost unnoticed. No special celebrations had marked New Year's Day, as all eyes were set on the next World's Fair—in French l'Exposition Universelle—due to open in the city in the spring. On that dull January 1 morning, Parisians who did not have to work headed for the Champ de Mars to check progress on the site. Elegant facades, domes and glinting glass, ornate ironwork, the Petit and Grand Palais emerged at the heart of Paris, a striking contrast to the straight austere lines of the resilient Eiffel Tower. Their smooth almost feminine curves seemed to mirror the sixteen-foot-high effigy of the fashionable Parisienne greeting visitors at the fair's entrance. Over the next seven months, fifty million visitors, a world record at the time, filed through the gates to marvel at the scientific displays, the discoveries of Pasteur and the Curies, the exotic items from the colonies, and the must-haves of the new consumer age.

The Eiffel Tower from *Vues de Paris: Héliochromes* (opposite page, top left); La Porte Monumentale, from *Il y a 100 Ans: L'Europe d'Autrefois* (middle left); announcement from the *Paris Herald*, November 1899 (bottom left); the cover of *Encyclopedie du Siècle: Exposition de Paris 1900*, Montgredin et Cie (top right).

CITY ON THE MOVE

The city's most valuable legacy of the World's Fair was in the realm of public transport, which had to be modernized to cope with the expected numbers of visitors. The railway had made its first appearance in Paris in the 1830s, but its oldest station, the Gare de l'Est, was now renovated, and work started on the new Gare de Lyon and its restaurant, later known as Le Train Bleu, and famous to this day. On the Left Bank, where the Palais d'Orsay had been destroyed by fire during the Paris Commune of 1871, Victor Laloux, Lucien Mayne, and Emile Bénard built the Gare d'Orsay, the first electrified urban terminal in the world.

The idea of underground transport for Paris had been debated for several decades, but following a string of technical and financial setbacks, Paris lagged behind London and New York. The Exhibition was the perfect incentive, and the first underground electric line—then, as now, called Line 1—was opened in July 1900, linking Vincennes to Porte de Maillot, stopping several times on the Champs Élysées for the benefit of Exhibition visitors. Line 2, opened in 1900 and extended in 1903, ran through the northern parts of the city from Porte Dauphine to Nation, linking with Line 1 at both ends. From the start, the system was named after the company set up to run it, the Compagnie du Chemin de Fer Métropolitain de Paris, shortened to *le métropolitain* or, most commonly, *le métro*.

The new métro was feted by Parisians and visitors alike, who loved its modernity and efficiency. The dangers of underground travel were, however, brought home on the evening of August 10, 1903, when disaster struck on Line 2. Although smoke had been seen coming from under the lead car at Boulevard Barbès, an empty eastbound train was allowed to crawl toward the terminus at Nation while a triple load of passengers, many from earlier canceled trains, followed on train number 48.

As the stricken empty train limped past the station at Couronnes, the stationmaster was justifiably alarmed at the obvious signs of fire. By the time train 48 arrived a few minutes later, eddying smoke was visible in the tunnel ahead. Rather than pulling forward to the station exit as usual, the driver stopped his train halfway along the platform to consult with the stationmaster. With the danger finally understood, the decision was made to evacuate to the street—but by now the passengers were becoming uncooperative. Fare refunds were being demanded and a lively altercation ensued; then suddenly it was too late. Couronnes station was plunged into darkness as a dense, choking cloud of smoke billowed from the tunnel. In less than a minute the station had become a death trap; disoriented by the smoke and far from the exit, eighty-four people died.

Within a week, safety measures were put in place; multiunit train control would follow later, further reducing the risk of fire, and, after the initial shock, Parisians returned to the métro, symbol of the future for an unstoppable city. In a decade or so, the number of journeys increased from 55 million a year to 500 million. The métropolitain ran almost entirely underground, the only visible impact on the streets being the entrances designed by Hector Guimard, a major protagonist of French Art Nouveau, or *style moderne*. Functional yet pleasing to the eye, the *bouches du métro* sprouted wrought-iron gates and canopies like giant bouquets of flowers and foliage, adding a graceful touch to the broad straight boulevards designed by Baron Haussmann.

To cope with increasing traffic aboveground, more bridges were built across the Seine—Pont Debilly (1900), Pont de Bir Hakeim (1903–5), and Pont Alexandre III (1896–1900), inaugurated for the Exposition and named in honor of the tsar and the Franco-Russian Alliance.

Front page of *Petit Parisien*, Sunday, August 23, 1903—*The Initial Rescue* (top); a modern photograph of a typical Art Deco métro entrance (below).

An 1895 poster for Cycles Gladiator by "Misti" (top left); lady cyclist from the *New York Herald*, July 20, 1896 (top right); a 1906 postcard of Maison Renault (middle); a 1908 postcard of a Paris autobus (bottom).

Spanning the river from the Champs Élysées to the Invalides, graced by winged horses, cherubs, and nymphs, it was the most glorious of them all.

The first automobiles seen in the city had been the privilege of a few—custom-built with a two-year wait for delivery—but by 1909 Paris had over 1,500 motorized taxis and its first buses. Along with steam—and later electric—streetcars, they quickly overtook horse-drawn omnibuses. The Renault factory, established in 1899 in the suburb of Billancourt, was by 1909 producing relatively affordable cars at the rate of more than 5,000 a year. In the early days of the automobile, France led the way in car racing, staging city-to-city rallies and the first Grand Prix in 1906, but in the following year the acme of races, the Peking to Paris, was won by an Italian vehicle. For the middle classes who preferred freedom to public transport, bicycles became increasingly popular.

By 1909 the improved infrastructure brought visitors from across Europe and beyond to a city that epitomized progress and pleasure. It also enabled people from the provinces to travel to Paris to see the sights or look for work, and the Parisians to enjoy a day out in the country or head for Deauville and the beach. Moreover, it meant that industry could now relocate to the outskirts, taking advantage of available space and cheaper rents while satisfying the fast-increasing demand for consumer goods.

Three main areas were targeted for industrial development—Canal Saint Denis and the Villette Basin to the northeast, Javelle and Grenelle to the southwest, and Picpus, Charonne, and Bercy to the southeast. More developments occurred beyond the old Thiers fortifications. Many artisans continued

to work in the city, but between 1860 and 1914 the population in the *banlieue* tripled, swollen by large numbers of rural and foreign migrants. Immigration itself caused little concern, especially as the birthrate was falling, but housing was poor, often without running water or decent sanitation. The Confédération Générale du Travail, which soon became France's most influential trades union, was founded in 1895. It found fertile ground in these swarming suburbs, its activities defining the rift between the political right and left. This chasm was further accentuated by the official separation of church and state in 1905, and reinforced by the establishment of a unified Socialist Party under Jean Jaurès.

THE NEW FACE OF PARIS

As workers moved out to the suburbs, Paris's privileged elite—Le Monde—relaxed in the stylish and spacious quarters created under the auspices of Napoléon III. Gone were the narrow winding lanes, along with the worst of the slums, which had sheltered the poorest of the poor. Renaissance mansions and medieval houses that had stood in the way had fallen to the vision of the "demolition artist," as Baron Haussmann, the planner of the new Paris, designated himself. Three hundred and fifty thousand people were displaced as the new boulevards took shape. The old romantics lamented the loss of the city's soul, but there were fortunes to be made for developers. There were now wide streets to enable the rapid deployment of troops in case of unrest. There were pleasing vistas, straight roads, and apartments festooned with balconies for the new bourgeoisie.

Against this elegant background, Guimard's florid entrances to the métro may have raised some eyebrows, but the 1900 Exposition acted as a catapult for his innovative architectural style. The past was gone, the future was bright, and Art Nouveau came into fashion. Society was ready for change. Haussmann's uniform rows of apartment blocks now appeared dull rather than harmonious, and new building regulations began to encourage the development of "picturesque tendencies." Bow windows and rococo embellishments made a bold appearance, roof space was converted into extra floors, and an annual prize was awarded for the best facade. Inspired by the exuberance of the natural world, Art Nouveau was all about new ideas and materials—glass, iron, and steel, with plenty of color and natural light, functional and cheap enough for the benefit of the masses.

The last decade of the nineteenth century and the first of the twentieth saw an army of talented architects take on the challenge of redesigning Paris—Hector Guimard, Frantz Jourdain, Henri Sauvage, Charles Plumet, and Paul Auscher. Crowds marveled at Guimard's new Castel Béranger apartments on Rue de la Fontaine, Sauvage's low-cost apartment building on Rue de la Chine, completed in 1907, and the ornate Trémois Building in the Rue Agar. With the convenience of elevators, living on the upper floors of buildings away from the noise and pollution of street level became more popular. The fashionable districts of Chaillot, Passy, and Auteuil were transformed.

Restaurants and cafés with Art Nouveau exteriors and decor sprang up, from the Café de Paris to Lucas Carlton and Maxim's. Multistoried department stores—*les grands magasins*—followed suit. The new Galeries Lafayette and Au Printemps, the extended Samaritaine, as vast as churches, took up the Art Nouveau theme, with their majestic staircases and galleries flooded with light.

FASHION

Elaborate or simplified, the *style moderne* touched every aspect of life—architecture, interior decoration, furniture, decorative arts, textiles, and fashion. For the wealthy Parisienne eager to shine and outdo her rival at the next ball, nothing mattered more than fashion. She went to great lengths to woo her dressmaker, smiling when she was kept waiting for an entire afternoon, hoping that a secret special to her might be revealed before "varnishing day." Even more important was the milliner, whose stunning creations were considered works of art, likened to "poems in ribbons and flowers."

A fashionable lady would own a range of dresses for all occasions, changing up to five times a day. If she had a dog, and many did, then there would also be a complete pet wardrobe in matching colors. At the top

of the market, those most able to impress had anklets incrusted with precious stones, fur-trimmed coats, and several silk umbrellas for rainy days. Royalty and the stars patronized Jean Worth and Madame Paquin in the Rue de la Paix, while the not-so-wealthy looked for ready-made imitations in the department stores. Men remained fairly conservative, choosing to assert their individuality with mustaches and beards of every description.

The feminine silhouette that emphasized a woman's curves remained popular until around 1908, with the skirt to the ground, high-necked bodices, and hats with elaborate flowers and plumes. By 1909, however, simpler designs and more experimental outfits were making an appearance, mirroring the transition through Art Nouveau to Art Deco. By 1906 there was a clear shift

Le Grand Lac, Bois de Boulogne, from the *New York Herald*, August 1901 (top); hat *c.* 1900, from *La Mode Illustré*; *Les Modes Femines du XIXieme* by Henri Boutet, *c.* 1900 (bottom).

LE MATIN AUX ACACIAS. ✳ MORNING SCENE IN THE BOIS.
By L. SABATTIER.

Marie Curie in a 1910 photograph (top left); *Le Matin aux Acacias*, from the fashion supplement of the *New York Herald*, May 29, 1910 (top right); an 1899 drawing by Harry Abrams (above); a 1905 postcard of Sarah Bernhardt (below).

EQUAL BUT DIFFERENT

Fronted by its giant statue of a fashionable Parisienne and a bronze chariot led by triumphant women, the 1900 Exposition had in many respects been a celebration of women. For the most part, Parisiennes were happy in their role, considering themselves on par with men in their social and intellectual life, and any call for change concentrated on small but significant issues, such as the right to vote in local elections or retaining their share of the marriage estate after a divorce.

In 1897 Marguerite Durand had founded the first feminist daily paper, *La Fronde*, and the start of the century was marked by a number of important changes. In 1900 the ban on women lawyers was lifted, and in 1905 the magazine *La Vie Heureuse* inaugurated the Femina literary prize, open to both sexes but judged by an all-female jury presided over by the novelist Anna de Noailles, the first woman to receive the Légion d'Honneur and one of the few to befriend the lesbian writer Colette. In 1906 the Nobel Prize-winning scientist Marie Curie was allowed to lecture at the University of Paris, and in 1907 a law was passed giving women sole right to their earnings. Three years later women were given eight weeks' unpaid maternity leave. Few Parisiennes, however, approved of the vociferous London suffragettes, aiming instead for the French Association pour les Droits des Femme's motto of "equality in dissimilarity."

Since the early 1880s, primary education had been available to all Parisians, and the ranks of self-made men were gradually swollen by middle-class women opting to go to work. Many headed for shops and offices, but the more ambitious joined the ranks of doctors and lawyers. Nothing could stop the steady rise of career women, though their male companions sometimes lamented the fact that, as contemporary historian Louis Gillet wrote, they should "become cogs in the social machine when, in fact, they are society's soul and conscience."

in favor of small hats, and in 1909 Parisian hairdresser Antoine invented the bob, giving the modern young Parisienne the sleek Joan of Arc look.

In the meantime, Paris had discovered the young fashion designer Paul Poiret, who in 1900 had designed the costumes for Sarah Bernhardt in Edmond Rostand's celebrated play *l'Aiglon*, introducing the scarf tied around the waist in oriental fashion. In 1903 he opened his own fashion house, where the actress Réjane was a regular visitor. These stars in the social firmament had the power to launch any fashion, and rarely paid for their gowns. For his petite and slender wife, Denise, Poiret developed what came to be known as the *garçonne* look. The familiar S-shape turned into a straight line, emphasized by a long jacket and domed hat with a brim. At the same time, Poiret mixed bright colors and pastel shades, presenting his creations in outdoor parades and producing a luxury *Robes de Poiret* catalog.

Meanwhile, the Comtesse de Béarn and many other Parisian hostesses continued to indulge in an all-consuming social life of fancy balls, coming-of-age parties, return *visites de digestion* to be paid exactly a week after an event, formal "at homes" to entertain the likes of Ravel or Isadora Duncan. More often than not in these circles, marriage was by arrangement, and gentle persuasion was brought to bear on a dutiful daughter. The brightest girls were sent to an all-female lycée, maybe even university, but singing and playing the piano remained as important as the art of intelligent conversation.

Following the flamboyant example of Sarah Bernhardt, these elegant Parisiennes did all they could to preserve their good looks. They gave up sweets, coffee, and tea, as advised by the diva's dietician, smoothed away cellulite with new electric gadgets, bathed in hyssop and oatmeal, and freshened up their complexion by riding through the avenues of the Bois de Boulogne.

THE BOULEVARDS

If you simply wanted a little life and company on your outings, you could stroll along the boulevards— "boulevards for the rich, boulevards for the poor, boulevards of every kind," wrote Dorothy Menpes in 1909. The Champs Elysées had long been fashionable, but now the Tout Paris could be seen parading from the Rue Drouot to the Rue Royale and along the Avenue de l'Opéra, built at the astronomical cost of 45 million francs. Who wanted to stay at home when there was so much to see—ladies parading the latest fashions, gentlemen reading the morning paper under the striped awning of a café terrace, friends meeting friends, eccentrics in felt hats and square-toed boots, traders, entrepreneurs, free spirits wandering from morning to night?

Armed with their *Baedeker*, Thomas Cook's agents herded bemused tourists around Notre Dame in fifteen minutes, but Parisians always had time to sit and stare, marvel at fountains and statues, or listen to the birds in the trees. One might spot a family huddled on a bench, just arrived from the provinces, mesmerized by the soldiers marching down the road or the young ladies stepping daintily out of carriages in the endless commotion of traffic.

The new streets ran straight as a ruler, lined with newspaper kiosks, columns covered in bright advertisements, bars, luxury shops, and department stores, where crowds from all walks of life gazed at the goods beautifully displayed in the windows. Inside, prices were fixed and clearly indicated, and whether you could afford it or not, you could try on the dress of your dreams. As befitted the Third Republic, such stores catered to all: the serious customer, the impulse buyer, the rich, and the not-so-rich.

To Parisians, the boulevards were more than just thoroughfares leading to a destination. They were life itself, shared by the dwindling number of aristocrats out to see and be seen, the bourgeoisie keen to emulate their lifestyle but proud to be different, and the workers eking out a living. Among them were the ever-resourceful street vendors, selling anything from mechanical toys to maps and toothpicks, errand girls carrying fabulous gowns across the city, bakers' boys delivering freshly baked loaves, sandwich men with their heads barely peeping above advertising boards, maids hurrying to market at the crack of dawn,

La Porte et le Boulevard Saint-Denis from *Vues de Paris*, c. 1906 (above); *Les Boulevards*, a postcard from c. 1902 (below); "Le Photographe," from *Scènes Parisiennes*, 1910 (bottom).

tripe sellers with jingling bells, fried-potato women huddled in doorways, and on Sundays the goatherd playing a flute on his rounds with goats and cart. You could buy butter wrapped in cabbage leaves, sausages and chickens, and even diamonds "better than the real thing." Down by the river, secondhand books tumbled from rickety stalls, women pushed carts filled with mussels, men unloaded wood, coal, sand, stones, bricks, grain, and wine. The *marchande de petit noir* prepared coffee on the quay, and barbers and dogshavers set up shop under the bridges.

THE GOOD LIFE

On a bright Sunday morning, the Seine came into its own. Rich and poor alike lined up for the steamers, bright-eyed and joyful at the prospect of a day out in the country. Almost anyone could afford the five-centime ride to Belle Vue. Before long they were gliding under the bridges, waving to stern-looking fishermen disentangling their lines, squeezing along the seats at each landing stage to make room for a gaggle of students or a family struggling with a baby, several toddlers, and a dog.

Soon the city was left behind, trees lined the banks, and now and then a rustic inn nestled in the greenery, strung with garlands of flags. They landed at Belle Vue to board the funicular railway, and the whole of Paris lay at their feet. There were strawberries and cakes in the café, flower gardens, and villas. When they went home tired but refreshed, clutching a few daisies or violets, myriad lights twinkled across the water.

Others boarded the streetcar on the Champ de Mars, which went all the way to Sceaux. They passed through the city gates

"Tondeur de chiens" (dog shaver), from *Paris Pittoresque* (above); "Palm Sunday," *Le Petit Journal*, April 9, 1911 (top right); 1901 Paris bus ticket and "Le Palais de Versailles, Chapel, Louis XV Wing" from *Souvenir de Paris et ses Environs* (below); "Jardin de Luxemborg—La Fontaine de Carpeaux" from *Paris*, by A. P. Etablissments Papeghin (bottom).

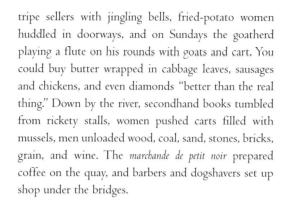

LE PALAIS DE VERSAILLES—AILE LOUIS XV—CHAPELLE

at Montrouge, clambering up and down hills until reaching the town, where every house was ready to serve food. There were donkey rides and roundabouts, or visitors could picnic in a tree house thirty feet above the ground. There was much laughter up there, especially among the young bohemians who descended with rosy cheeks and foliage in their hair.

Apart from the occasional outing to Versailles or Fontainebleau, the upper classes felt little need to leave their elegant quarters in the heart of the capital. If they wanted a change from the boulevards, they could always head for one of the parks. The working classes kept mostly to the Jardin des Plantes, to gape at stuffed animals and exotic creatures, so they would probably choose the Luxembourg or Tuileries Gardens. There, very proper ladies paraded in the Allée des Orangers, mothers brought daughters of marriageable age, and nannies kept an eye on their charges under the chestnut trees. There were hoops and skipping ropes, balloons, windmills, performing monkeys, and Guignol marionettes, swingboats, and wooden horses on a merry-go-round. They could sail model boats, or marvel at goldfish all the way from China in the marble pools.

The year was punctuated by festivities, from firework displays to Venetian carnivals, when huge crowds would gather on the riverbank. Every district

celebrated its saint's day with a fair, lotteries, shooting stalls, and roundabouts with bicycles, ostriches, and lions. There were festivals for Lent, Easter (when the crowds ate gingerbread), July 14 (with street dances in Republican fashion), Assumption Day (when young girls laid white flowers on the Virgin's altar), and All Saints' Day (when everyone honored their dead with potted chrysanthemums). Washerwomen held their own carnival, seamstresses had a holiday for St. Catherine's Fete, and New Year's Day meant presents for the coal man, the butcher's boy, and the lamplighter. Schoolchildren were treated to special outings free of charge as befitted a socialist state.

BOHEMIAN PARIS

"To breathe the air of Paris is to preserve the soul," wrote Victor Hugo, and for the bohemians of the early 1900s, art was the expression of the soul, the very purpose of life. Sharing cheap lodgings with like-minded spirits, dressed with complete disregard to fashion, they lived in the Latin Quarter around the Sorbonne and Montmartre. Here, radical feelings always ran high, stirred by memories of the brutally repressed commune uprising of 1871. Up on the hill, where a few windmills and vineyards survived, the gleaming new Basilica of Sacré-Coeur, commissioned by the government in 1873 as a symbol of hope and unity and completed only in 1914, was regarded as an insult rather than a gesture of reconciliation. By 1909, however, the revolutionary spirit of the young bohemians was generally limited to the rejection of bourgeois values, which, for many, had been the hallmark of their upbringing.

The group comprised artists, writers, philosophers, and disenchanted students united in their stand against conventional moral values and rising materialism. Seemingly afraid of nothing, they flaunted an alternative lifestyle, turning their poverty into a statement, devoting every moment to the pursuit of new ideas, pleasure, and art.

Many young women took advantage of this new freedom. Named after their cheap gray attire, the *grisettes* had left their middle-class comforts in search of freedom, working hard by day, enjoying heart-searching debates and male companionship by night. In cafés and bars, cheap restaurants, and brothels, the talk was of avant-garde and burning issues, fueled by tobacco smoke, absinthe, and opium.

Student remittances were spent within a few days, used to buy pâtisseries or flowers for a sweetheart, or to dine with friends in a proper restaurant with a tablecloth, maybe to sample a Russian dish at Noel and Peter's or one of the eighty egg courses at Chez Durand. In Montmartre, macabre was in fashion, with waiters dressed as devils or undertakers, and cabaret artists singing of murderers and thieves or staging mock executions. From the real-life gangs of "apaches" sporting red scarves and knives to the legendary antihero Fantômas, the underworld lurked in the dark alleys.

No one worried about tomorrow. Hopeful but penniless artists lived on soup, potatoes, and cheese, painting by night, toting their pictures by day around obscure galleries or trying to sell them on the Champs Élysées. On Saturday nights they drank until the early hours, discussing the merits of analytic shapes or primitive art, sometimes selling their work on the spot to pay the bill or, like Henri de Toulouse-Lautrec and Louise Weber—the cancan dancer La Goulue—promising future fame to a favorite

Sarah Bernhardt as Jeanne d'Arc, an 1893
poster by Eugène Grasset (right); Théâtrophone
(live telephone link to theater performances), an
1890 poster by Jules Chéret; a 1905 postcard of
Les Folies Bergère (bottom).

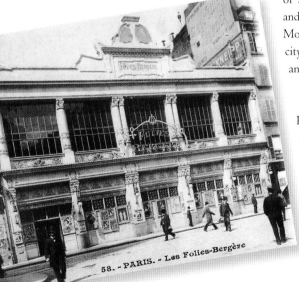

58. - PARIS. - Les Folies-Bergère

name of the French professional farter and entertainer
Joseph Pujol.

The Folies Bergère at 32 Rue Richer was a little
pricey at two francs a ticket, but, unlike upscale
theaters, you did not have to dress up or remove your
hat; you could come and go as you wished, smoke in the
corridor, and pick up a girl. The first shows included
circus acts such as clowns or the boxing kangaroo, but
by 1909 brilliant comedians like the young Charlie
Chaplin, cancan girls, and striptease shows had made
an appearance. Meanwhile, on the boulevards, the
popular farces of Georges Feydeau relentlessly poked
fun at the nouveaux riches.

More distinguished entertainment was on offer at
the Comédie-Française, also known as the Maison de
Molière, where lavish dinner parties were held on the
playwright's birthday. This was the refuge of good taste
and manners, where classics by Molière, Racine, and
Corneille were performed. The undisputed star of the
Parisian stage was Sarah Bernhardt, the "divine actress"
who captivated her audience not only with her talent—
whether playing the ailing Napoléon II or Joan of
Arc—but also with her unconventional lifestyle, refusing
to be tamed as she traveled across Europe and America,
courting the Prince of Wales, heir to the British throne,
and indulging in eccentricities like sleeping in a coffin.
Half a million Parisians went to the theater at least once
a week, and new phone booths offered a "theatrophone"
service where you could listen live to the plays being
performed in the boulevard theaters.

The real novelty of the time, however, was the
cinema, which provided cheap entertainment for the
masses. The Lumière brothers had held their first
moving picture show in the Grand Café in 1895, and
by 1914 Paris had thirty-seven cinemas, showing much
longer films than in the early days, from comedies to
dramas inspired by the novels of Victor Hugo and
Émile Zola. Hugo's *L'Assommoir* (*The Drunkard*), filmed
in 1909, portrayed the wretched life of a working-class
family, echoing the social unrest that had recently
brought workers out on strike across the country, from
wine growers and civil servants to railway workers and
Parisian builders.

model. They lived and played "in the serious service
of art," and many famous painters of the period lived
and worked in Montmartre—Henri Matisse, Amedeo
Modigliani, Pablo Picasso, and Georges Braque. The
city claimed a greater concentration of artists than
anywhere else in the world.

STAGE AND SCREEN

Paris in 1909 was a city of small stages, many
associated with cafés and restaurants. Such
establishments removed social barriers, at least
temporarily, offering cheap prices and pleasure for
everyone. Poems and rowdy songs mingled with
daring dances and political satire, or the antics
of the record-breaking Pétomane, the stage

La Rue de Javel – C. M.

Inondations de Paris
Janvier 1910

R. Baudouin

FLUCTUAT NEC MERGITUR

For the residents of northern France, the winter of 1909–10 was particularly hard. Heavy rainfall during January culminated in the worst floods that modern Paris has ever experienced. The Seine inundated streets throughout the city center, affecting thousands of homes and hundreds of businesses. The platforms at the new Gare d'Orsay were submerged and, as the water rose in the museum's basements, it was feared that priceless treasures in the Louvre would be lost forever.

The British journalist Warner Allen stood alongside a crowd that had gathered on one of the city's embankments and watched "the headlong rush of the silent yellow river that carried with it logs and barrels, broken furniture, the carcasses of animals, and perhaps sometimes a corpse, all racing madly to the sea." Paris began to look more like Venice as boats floated through the streets where buses and automobiles had traveled just days before. The government erected floating wooden walkways, and new ferry services were established to move people through the city. More than a million Parisians were evacuated; the cost of the floods was estimated at 400 million francs.

To many, the flood demonstrated the failure of the city's new infrastructure. Its modern sewage system was considered the best in the world, but it succumbed to the pressure of the floodwater. The new electric power station flooded, causing the innovative compressed air system that kept the city's public clocks synchronized to fail, meaning that they all stopped at exactly the same time—10:50 a.m. on January 21. Having no electric supply, the state-of-the-art métro was brought to a halt.

Parisians had discovered that there was much about their modern city that they could no longer depend on, but they did realize that they could still depend on one another. Paris survived the flood, not because it was a modern urban metropolis, but because it was a functioning human community. In its hour of need, Paris ceased to be a large city where people were anonymous and became a village of neighbors. As a journalist from the *New York Times* observed, "Parisians have taken the affliction with amazing fortitude; never has the solidarity of feeling of all the honest citizens been more apparent."

The Latin motto inscribed under the Paris coat of arms is *Fluctuat nec Mergitur*, "tossed by the waves, but not sunk," and much was made of the shared battle against the water. In the larger context, we now know that the citizens of Paris were to face a much larger and intractable foe just four years later, when Europe was plunged into the bloodiest war the continent had yet experienced. The sacred union—*l'union sacrée*—of the French people then faced an even greater battle, but maybe their battle against the rising Seine in 1910 had made Parisians just a little less complacent and a little more realistic about what it was possible to achieve when community, creativity, and technology are pushed to the limit.

Le Petit Journal

ADMINISTRATION
61, RUE LAFAYETTE, 61
Les manuscrits ne sont pas rendus
On s'abonne sans frais
dans tous les bureaux de poste

5 CENT. SUPPLÉMENT ILLUSTRÉ **5** CENT.

ABONNEMENTS

21me Année — Numéro 1.004

DIMANCHE 13 FÉVRIER 1910

FLUCTUAT NEC MERGITUR

DANS UN ÉLAN GÉNÉREUX, PARIS ET LA FRANCE ONT SECOURU LES INONDÉS

"Flooding in Rue de Javel," from *Inondations de Paris 1910*, with a cover designed by R. Baudouin (top); front cover of *Le Petit Journal*, February 13, 1910— "In a generous gesture, Paris and France have saved the victims of the floods."

MORTIMER MENPES
1855–1938

Self-portrait of Mortimer Menpes (above); Boer wagon commandeered and used by the Red Cross, from *War Impressions*, 1901.

Mortimer Menpes was the founding artist of A&C Black's series of color books, the first of which was published in 1901. It was his proposal for a book called *War Impressions*, based on his service as an artist for the magazine *Black and White* during the Boer War, that persuaded Adam Black to launch a project that led to the publication of several hundred lavishly illustrated books over the next two decades. Menpes contributed to more than twenty of these.

Menpes, describing himself in *Who's Who* many years later, when a certain vanity had pervaded his personality, said he was "inartistically born in Australia" in 1855 (not 1859 as he tried to pretend), and that he was "nominally educated at a grammar school in Port Adelaide, but really on a life scheme of his own. His career as a painter began when he was one year old." He describes himself as "painter, etcher, raconteur, and rifle shot," listing many one-man exhibitions of his work but omitting any mention of his wife and children.

In 1875 Menpes moved to London and married the eighteen-year-old Rosa Mary Grosse, who had also been born in Adelaide. By the early 1890s the couple had produced five children, not all of whom survived infancy, and Menpes's decision to work as a war artist in South Africa at the end of the decade suggests a certain detachment from his close family. However, his wife seems to have accompanied him on many of his other travels, and a description in the *Lady* on January 24, 1889, of the Little Miss Menpes's Ball at Osborne House, Munster Terrace, describes in mawkish detail the fancy dress worn by their daughter Maud and her siblings, suggesting a life not much different from other prosperous Victorian families.

In the 1870s Menpes studied at the South Kensington School of Design, and in 1880 he met James McNeill Whistler, leaving art school to study with him. Menpes's recollections of his time with Whistler were later published in his 1904 book *Whistler as I Knew Him*. Menpes was elected to the Royal Society of Painters and Etchers in 1881, and became a member of the Society of British Artists in 1885. In 1886 he was one of the founding members of the New English Art Club. In 1897 he was elected a member of the Institute of Painters in Water Colours, and in 1899 to the Institute of Oil Painters.

In 1887 Menpes went to study in Japan. When he returned, his Japanese paintings formed the first of many one-man exhibitions, held at the Dowdeswell Galleries in Bond Street, London. It caused a sensation in the art world, counting among its visitors Robert Browning, Oscar Wilde—to whose younger son, Vyvyan, Menpes was godfather—and even the Prince of Wales. All his pictures were sold, fetching a total of more than £2,000.

Something of Whistler's eccentricity seems to have rubbed off on Menpes, since C. R. W. Nevinson records in his book *Paint and Prejudice* that Cézanne, Van Gogh, and Gauguin had all presented canvases to Menpes, who, considering them the work of "ardent bunglers," put them aside and lost them.

Menpes's first book for A&C Black set the standard for many others. Published in an edition of 3,000 copies, it contained ninety-nine full-page illustrations in color produced by the recently invented mechanical three-color process, plus 63,000 words of text. A large limited edition of 350 copies carried the artist's signature. The book sold well and was reprinted in a slightly larger format, encouraging A&C Black to proceed with what turned out to be a lucrative venture.

Menpes's next volume was *Japan* (1901). Ever since his first visit to the country, Japan's influence had pervaded all aspects of his life, and his home in Cadogan Gardens just off Sloane Square was decorated in the Japanese style. The house was designed by A. H. Mackmurdo, and a full description entitled *An Experiment in the Application of Japanese Ornament to the Decoration of an English House* appeared in the *Studio* magazine in 1899. Among its features was a small mirror angled above one of the upper windows so that Menpes could scrutinize would-be visitors before deciding whether to be "at home" to them. The façade of this house remains and is incorporated into the northwest corner of the Peter Jones department store.

In the following years, Menpes, together with his elder daughter, Maud, founded and ran the Menpes Press. Among its achievements was a revolutionary new process for reproducing great paintings, which resulted in publication of *The Menpes Series of Great Masters*, a quantity of which were presented to the Australian government. Menpes continued to contribute to A&C Black's list, including *Brittany*, *The Durbar*, *India*, *Paris*, *The Thames*, *Venice*, *China*, and two compilations, *World Pictures* and *World's Children*.

In 1907 Menpes founded and ran the Menpes Fruit Farm at Pangbourne in Berkshire, and later he bought land in Purley, Surrey, to set up the Carnation Nurseries. He was joined in these ventures by his son Claude, who continued to run a fruit farm at Westwood Farm, Tilehurst, until his death in 1963.

For the last thirty years of his life, Mortimer Menpes lived at Iris Court, Pangbourne. Rosa Mary died on August 23, 1936, and Mortimer on April 1, 1938. Both were buried in Pangbourne, and memorials can be found in the churchyard. In 1984 Menpes Close in Purley was named after Mortimer. Of Menpes's children, Maud remained unmarried; Mortimer James died young; Walter, at some time an actor, died in 1945, after which his widow (according to Dorothy Menpes's daughter-in-law) jumped to her death from the top of Swan and Edgar's department store in London's Regent Street.

Mortimer Menpes was a man of many parts—artist, engraver, printer, traveler, raconteur, farmer. He made a lasting impact in the fields of etching, printmaking, and color reproduction of paintings. His obituary in the *Times* summed him up with the words, "Menpes made a much greater impression as a personality that as an artist, being alert, resourceful and opportunist—never at a loss for a retort in argument." But without his vision and energy, A&C Black's color books might never have met with the resounding success that they did.

His paintings can be found in galleries in Australia, New Zealand, San Francisco, and Glasgow, and in the Tate Gallery in London. His work is widely collected, with individual paintings fetching well into five figures.

Umbrellas and Commerce, from *Japan*, 1901 (top);
A Pink Palace, from *Venice*, 1904 (above);
Mortimer Menpes's signature (below).

PLATE 1

A KIOSK ON THE BOULEVARD

Parisians have always been great newspaper readers, reading the front pages
pasted to advertising columns as well as buying their own copy.

The word "boulevard" indicates an elegantly wide road, and in Paris the general rule is that boulevards encircle the city while avenues radiate from the center. The most famous Parisian boulevards, dating from the Haussmann reconstruction between 1853 and 1870, were often referred to collectively as Les Grands Boulevards.

During the 1850s and 1860s, there were so many theaters showing plays based on dreadful crime stories that the Grands Boulevards were sometimes known as "les boulevards du crime." On the Boulevard du Temple, some actors were "killed" 11,000 times, and one famous actress was the victim of 8,000 seductions! Real-life crime was common in the area too, as mafia elements from Sicily, Marseilles, and Corsica used the Grands Boulevards as their preferred midnight playground.

Newspapers, especially weeklies like *Le Petit Parisien* and *Le Petit Journal* with their color sections, were a popular source of education and entertainment, regularly featuring gory scenes of true crime and terrible accidents.

The Grands Boulevards were among the first streets to accommodate the famous columns on which the cover page of each newspaper was pasted each day. Since 1840, the typically Parisian green wooden benches had multiplied everywhere in the city, including the Grands Boulevards. Everything was organized to attract people to the streets, so much so that Yves Montand, one of France's most famous singers, was to write an anthem to the Grands Boulevards, in which he sang of his affection for the constantly evolving and entertaining life of the Paris streets. For him, there was no greater pleasure in Paris than to lose himself in the crowds of the city's working people.

PLATE 2

CURIOSITY

A crowd gathers to see a *cabinet de curiosités*—perhaps some giant fossils,
an extinct animal, or a rare collection of strange tropical plants.

In this colorful painting, Menpes conveys the excitement the crowd must have felt when presented with some strange creature, or a collection of exotic objects from Egypt, Turkey, or even farther afield. The *boulevardiers*, the habitués of the Grands Boulevards, were always ready to be awed and amazed by bizarre and out-of-the-way spectacles.

The word "boulevard" is derived from the medieval word *bulwerc* or "bulwark," as the Grands Boulevards were built on the site of the old Paris ramparts. The Grands Boulevards as Menpes knew them were a recent addition to the Paris landscape, being the main plank in the plans drawn up by Georges Haussmann to modernize the city in the 1860s and 1870s. They extended in a long arc from the Église de la Madeleine in the west to the Bastille in the east.

The streets off the Grands Boulevards constituted the city's main commercial and financial district, with institutions such as the Banque de France and the Bourse, and the glittering Opéra Garnier. Scattered around the Grands Boulevards area were many delightful passages—arcades with glass roofs and tiled floors. Perhaps the best known, Passage Jouffroy, was built in 1847 and was one of the first heated shopping galleries in Paris. These peaceful passages are now, as in Menpes's time, a pleasant way to pass the time window-shopping and admiring the architecture, especially when the weather is cold and wet.

LES JOUETS DE L'ANNÉE ET L'AFFAIRE HUMBERT

PLATE 3

NOTRE DAME

The Cathedral of Notre Dame hovers like a gigantic spider over the Île de la Cité.

The church's graceful flying buttresses demonstrate one of the key innovations of Gothic architecture, developed in the twelfth century. At this time the Roman style, with its heavy stone walls, small windows, and rounded arches, began to give way to the flamboyance of lighter walls and fiery stained-glass windows rising to incredible heights. These architectural innovations and the pointed, narrow Gothic arch were all made possible by the support provided by flying buttresses.

Notre Dame has had a somewhat checkered history. In its early years it was an inspiring setting for the crowning of kings and the blessing of Crusaders. Later, during the French Revolution, it was ransacked, and the heads in the Kings' Gallery, which actually represent the kings of Judea and Israel, Christ's forebears, were mistaken for the kings of France and shattered.

In 1831, when Victor Hugo, one of France's most important authors, wrote *The Hunchback of Notre Dame*, popular feeling arose in support of the restoration of the church. Starting in 1845, the architect Eugène Viollet-le-Duc worked for twenty-three years to restore the statuary, stained glass, doors, and spire.

Like the woman in the painting, no one passing behind the cathedral can resist the temptation to stand and gaze as it rises delicately out of the morning mist.

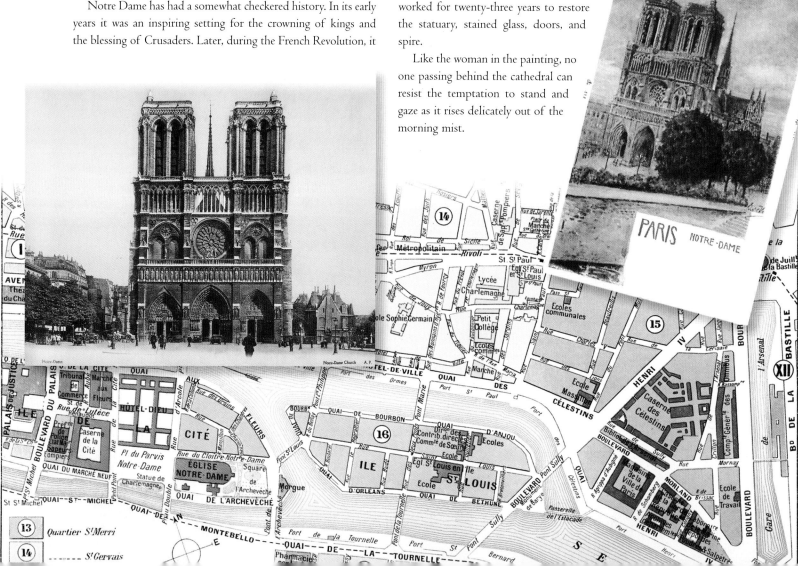

PLATE 4

THE LAWNS IN THE TUILERIES

The Tuileries Garden gets its name from its clay soil, which was used to make tiles, or *tuiles*.

Catherine de Médicis, queen consort of King Henry II from 1547 to 1559, created an Italian-style park on this site in 1563, but a century later the gardens were suffering from serious neglect. Jean-Baptiste Colbert, finance minister under Louis XIV, the Sun King, had the prolific French seventeenth-century architect André Le Nôtre redesign the garden, which is still preserved today, the oldest French-style garden in Paris.

Here Menpes has focused on the architect's magnificent vistas of lawns and flower beds, backed by the quintessentially Parisian garden backdrop of tall chestnuts. The painting shows one of the gardens' many white marble sculptures. The older statues witnessed many terrible events during the French Revolution, including the sacking of the nearby Tuileries Palace on August 10, 1792, when the gardens were strewn with more than a thousand corpses.

By the 1900s, however, the park had become a peaceful place to stroll, or to contemplate the harmonious spaces and bright green lawns from the chairs provided by the City of Paris—though you had to pay to sit on them. Pride of place in the Tuileries Gardens is now given to several large bronze sculptures of generously proportioned women by the Catalan sculptor Aristide Maillol, placed there by André Malraux, then Minister of Culture, in 1964.

PLATE 5

AFTERNOON ON THE SEINE

Menpes, as this painting so tellingly demonstrates, was a protégé of the artist James McNeill Whistler.

Like his teacher and friend Whistler, who was famous for his atmospheric renderings of the Thames in London, Menpes here captures the glowing late-afternoon light with Impressionistic freedom and fervor.

The bridge was originally to be called the Pont des Saints-Pères, as it was an extension of the Rue des Saint-Pères, but at its inauguration in 1834, King Louis XVI of France christened it the Pont du Carrousel. Its architect, Antoine-Rémy Polonceau, used an innovative lightweight structure of timber and cast iron, creating Paris's first three-arched iron bridge. The distinctive iron circles that decorate the structure of the three arches were affectionately dubbed "napkin rings." At each corner of the bridge was set a sculpture by Petitot Louis, portraying Abundance, Industry, the Seine, and the City of Paris.

Half a century later the bridge required major repairs, and in 1906 the timber deck was replaced with iron. Despite this, the bridge was still deemed too narrow for road traffic and too low for river navigation. In 1930 the bridge shown here was demolished and a new stone structure built a little downstream. The architects, Malet and Lang, strove to retain the general shape of the original bridge, and incorporated an ingenious system of telescopic lampposts, now sadly out of service.

PLATE 6

IN THE SQUARE OF THE HÔTEL DE VILLE

Civic ceremonies regularly take place in the large open square in front of the Hôtel de Ville.

In Menpes's painting, as we look across to the row of shops and cafés lining the north side of the square, the space in front of the Hôtel de Ville is almost empty, which suggests it is early morning.

This square was originally called the Place de Grève, *grève* meaning both "shore" and "strike"—this was where out-of-work laborers came to find a job. During the *ancien régime*, it was also the site of public executions and is famous for being the place where the guillotine was first used, to the disappointment of a crowd accustomed to somewhat more protracted forms of execution.

By 1803 the square had been renamed Place de l'Hôtel de Ville, and in 1852 Xavier Ruel, a businessman from Lyon, started a small store like those we see here under the striped red awnings. In 1855 he was instrumental in saving the life of Empress Eugénie when her horses bolted, and was awarded a sum of money for his heroic act, which he promptly invested in a larger property. In 1912 the Bazaar de l'Hôtel de Ville, usually shortened to BHV, was revamped and crowned by the famous rotunda. Today many events are organized in the square, including an ice-skating rink in the winter and a volleyball court in the summer.

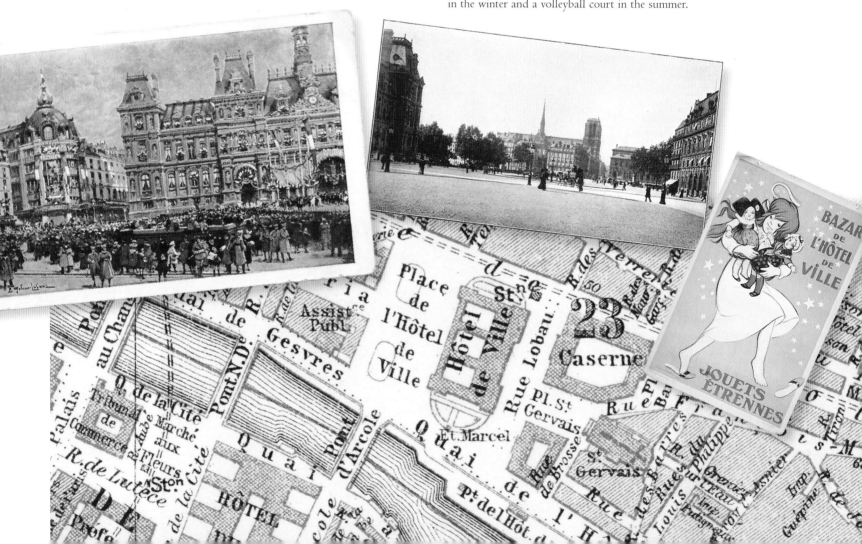

PLATE 7

RUE DE LA FAYETTE

Then, as now, French cooking depended on the availability of high-quality fresh produce.

Here again are Paris's ubiquitous fruit carts, but the dress shop behind the street vendors indicates that we are in a relatively upscale part of the city. In fact, the internationally renowned department store Galeries Lafayette is very close to the street of the same name, both being named after the Marquis de la Fayette, the Franco-American hero who fought against the English during the American Revolution. A spokesman for free-thinking French aristocrats, he survived the French Revolution and was one of the authors of the *Declaration of the Rights of Man*. He would probably turn in his grave if he knew that his name had become synonymous with an iconic shopping mecca.

The Rue Lafayette, one of the longest streets in Paris at 1.7 miles, is always crowded, lined as it is with cafés, bars, brasseries, and boutiques. The Café du Croissant, a brasserie on a corner of the Rue Montmartre, is famous for witnessing the assassination of the socialist politician Jean Jaurès on July 13, 1914. He was quietly eating a strawberry tart when an antipacifist, who believed that France should fight to take Alsace–Lorraine back from the Germans, shot three bullets into his body. The crowd that always frequented this part of Paris surrounded the café crying "Vive Jaurès" as reporters raced to the scene from the offices of the city's many newspapers to cover the story.

This incident is typical of paradoxical Paris—casual, imaginative, fickle, head in the clouds, but always alert to the excitement of a political headline.

JAURÈS.— Au Meeting du Pré St Gervais

PLATE 8

PONT DE TOLBIAC

Wine-colored clouds gather over a scene that has seen many changes since it was painted a hundred years ago.

The Pont de Tolbiac was built in 1879 as part of a Parisian urbanization program, connecting the Rue de Tolbiac on the Left Bank with the Rue de Dijon, which used to service the Bercy warehouses, the center of the Paris wine business. Today the area has been restored as a garden, preserving the old trees watching over the storehouses that, when Menpes painted the scene, housed thousands of barrels of wine.

The nearby Port de Tolbiac, which handles 280,000 tons of river traffic every year, is currently undergoing reconstruction, part of a plan to enhance the eastern part of the city while preserving its economic vitality in a sustainable way, water being a more ecologically sound method of transportation than road or rail.

The well-known French mystery author Léo Malet has been inspired by mist-covered views of the bridge to make it a setting for many a nefarious deed. The bridge also leads to the Bibliothèque Nationale de France François Mitterand, the new national library, opened in 1996 and named in honor of France's famous socialist president. The four great book-shaped towers house over ten million volumes; scholars work in an underground setting lined with exotic woods, harnessing the latest in modern computer technology.

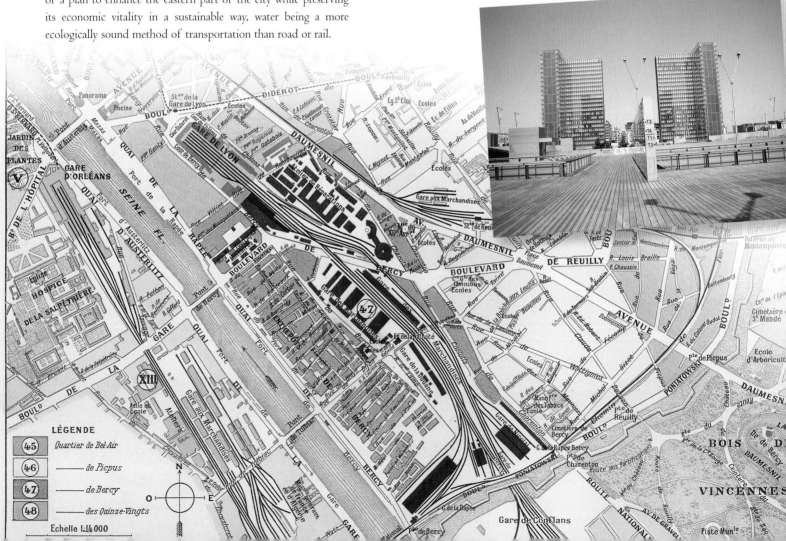

PLATE 9

HÔTEL DE VILLE

The trees have disappeared, but the facade of Paris's town hall has not changed since the seventeenth century.

The first Hôtel de Ville, known as "The House of Pillars," was built in the thirteenth century for the city's provost of merchants, who ruled the markets for the guilds. This was replaced by a palace designed by Il Boccadoro, an Italian architect. Construction began in 1533 and was completed in 1628. Extensions added between 1836 and 1850 preserved the Renaissance facade of highly ornate stonework, turrets, and statues overlooking the famous square we see in the painting.

The worker-led revolution of May 1871 reduced the palace to cinders, along with the city's archives, but the Hôtel de Ville was reconstructed between 1874 and 1882 with an identical Renaissance facade, adorned with statues representing such French luminaries as the philosopher Théodore Rousseau, the writer and political thinker Voltaire, the novelist and essayist Madame de Staël, and Charles Le Brun, the seventeenth-century painter who decorated much of the Palace of Versailles. Other statues represent important French towns. The entire effect is typical of the official style of the early years of the Third Republic.

Today, modern illuminated fountains welcome guests at the elaborate banquets regularly hosted at the Hôtel de Ville by Paris's mayor.

PLATE 10

HOUSES AND SHOPS ON THE SEINE

Fortunate indeed is the householder whose windows look out onto the river.

For the most part, central Paris is a mixture of residential and business districts, and the streets lining the banks of the Seine as it flows through the heart of the city have always been some of the most desirable locations to live and work.

Here the bridge—almost certainly the north end of the Pont Louis Philippe—is deserted, but even in 1909 this was a rare sight, as a constant flow of pedestrians, carriages, omnibuses, and early automobiles crowded across the river from dawn until late into the night. Today the situation is even worse as cars and tourist buses clog Paris's main river crossings.

The Impressionist painter Henri Matisse lived in an apartment overlooking the Seine, where he executed his famous Fauve paintings of *péniches*, the heavy barges gliding down the river. So did his friend Albert Marquet, who later deserted the Fauve movement to paint subtle, rich, gray-toned pictures of the Seine docks.

Menpes here gives us a glimpse of some of Paris's charming cast-iron streetlights, previously gaslit but by 1909 wired for electricity. Paris first adopted municipal gas lighting in 1818, each lamp being lit by a lamplighter every evening, and for the following century the city was probably the best lit in the world, earning it the nickname of "Ville-Lumière," or City of Light.

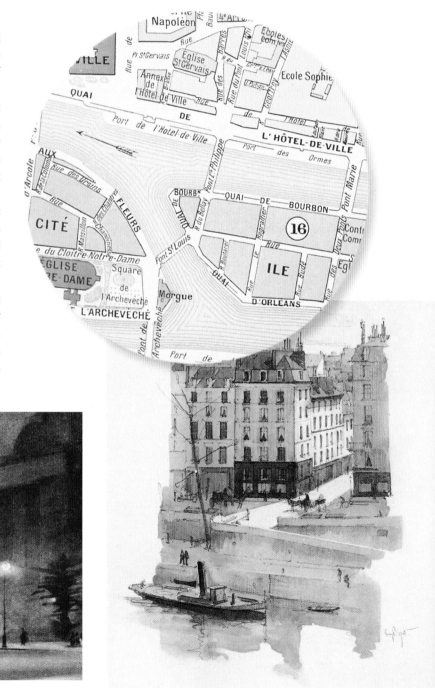

PLATE 11

LA SAMARITAINE

Named after the pump by the Pont Neuf, which supplied water to the center of Paris,
La Samaritaine was one of the first of a new type of shop, the department store, or *grand magasin*.

The brainchild of entrepreneur Ernest Cognacq, the first Samaritaine opened its doors in 1869. The shop comprised a single room, which Cognacq rented at forty-five francs a day. Cognacq's wife, Marie-Louise Jaÿ, was the first saleswoman. The shop's main innovations—fixed, displayed prices and the opportunity to try on clothes before buying them—proved very popular, and by 1909 this *grand magasin* had a grand reputation to match its grand name, and had expanded considerably in size. Sales rocketed in the early years of the century, from a turnover of just over six million francs a year in 1900 to nearly one billion francs in 1915.

Thirty years after it opened, the store of Menpes's painting had to be replaced by a new building. Completed in 1910, its metallic structure with large bay windows was revolutionary. When the second store was constructed in 1928, the management wanted a stone facade, so architects Henri Sauvage and Frantz Jourdain designed a metallic structure clad with Art Deco sculptures. Much of the interior has also been preserved, including the Art Nouveau ironwork staircase and the stained glass.

The *grands magasins* changed how people shopped, passing control from old-fashioned shopkeepers directly into the hands of customers. They gave author Émile Zola new social groups to analyze— the male manager preying on the poor salesgirls; the wealthy woman who, despite her money, is overcome by kleptomania.

In 2001, following several years of financial difficulties, the store was bought by the Louis Vuitton–Moët Hennessy group. In June 2005 it closed "in order to bring it up to date with stringent safety standards." Many people believe that it may never open as a department store again.

PLATE 12

FOUNTAINS AT VERSAILLES

The fountains are the central feature of the famous gardens commissioned by Louis XIV.

When the Sun King commissioned André Le Nôtre, the great French landscape architect, to redesign the gardens of the royal palace at Versailles, one of his specific requests was a fountain honoring Apollo, Greek god of the sun. The painting shows the fulfilment of his request, a sculpture designed by Jean-Baptiste Tuby. Apollo is portrayed in gold-covered lead, rising from the sea into the sky, drawn by his horses. In 1909 the fountain was showing its age; today's visitors can see the fountain restored to its former bright glory.

Le Nôtre transformed the gardens into the geometric paths and shrubberies typical of the French formal garden, and the work was completed in 1668. It was the Italian engineer Agostino Ramelli who developed the water-driven pumps that made it possible to build and maintain the spectacular water gardens with their many fountains.

Versailles' gardens enjoyed spectacular success, influencing landscape artists throughout Europe. In Menpes's painting, glimpses of the tall trees in the background tantalize us with their carefully cropped forms typical of the period, and it is possible to imagine the ghost of Marie Antoinette sketching, as was seen in the gardens by two English women, Anne Moberly and Eleanor Jourdain, in 1901. Principal and vice-principal of Saint Hugh's College, Oxford, the two academics became well-known for their "Ghosts of Versailles." They later published their experiences of the haunting—under the pseudonyms of Miss Morison and Miss Lamont—in a 1911 book entitled *An Adventure*.

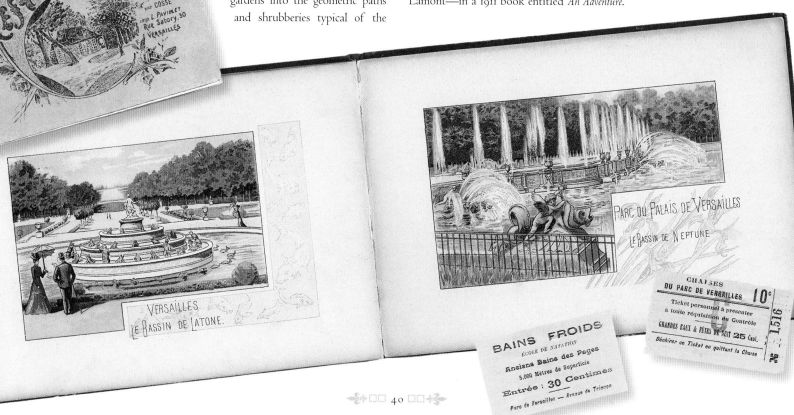

PLATE 13

AU BORD DE LA SEINE

The Pont Louis Philippe and Église Saint-Gervais-Saint-Protais are framed
in that quintessential Parisian combination of sunlight and gray sky.

The woman in black with the pink parasol, adding a note of color to the otherwise low-key harmony of the scene, is possibly about to cross the bridge to attend mass. The church on the other side of the river, usually referred to as the Église Saint-Gervais, is most famous for having been the church in which the

Couperin musical dynasty played and composed. In 1685 François Couperin inherited the post of organist from his father, Louis, and when he retired the honor passed to his cousin Nicolas. For two generations, the Couperins composed works for a remarkable organ that is still being played today. We can imagine the woman in black entering the church to the resonant strains of that great instrument and walking quietly to a pew or kneeling before the central altar lit by dozens of candles.

Behind the church rises the Tour Saint Jacques, the only remaining vestige of the thirteenth-century Église Saint Jacques de la Boucherie, the traditional starting point of that long, exhausting, and sometimes dangerous pilgrimage to the Cathedral of Santiago de Compestela in northern Spain. The journey from what is now just a tower to the tomb of Saint James, the apostle of Christ, attracts even more pilgrims today than it did a hundred years ago.

PLATE 14

BOOKSTALL ON THE SEINE

Many a bookworm with a few sous to spend has enjoyed a pleasant hour exploring the stalls along the riverside.

The bookstalls in the painting, across the river from the west wing of the Louvre, are still an important part of life in Paris. Their black metal boxes—today they are green—were attached to the waist-high walls that line the river through the Latin Quarter. In the 1900s they offered schoolbooks, dictionaries, volumes of sermons, biographies, histories, and French classics; and priests like the one portrayed by Menpes would join students and scholars to spend sunny afternoons browsing in hope of unearthing a rare treasure.

Ernest Hemingway, American expatriate novelist, short-story writer, and journalist, and the senior member of the famous "Lost Generation" that also included such luminaries as Gertrude Stein and James Joyce, made a science of finding quality works by determining which bookstalls sold books purchased from employees working in luxury hotels.

The booksellers, or *bouquinistes*, are obliged by law to open their stalls a minimum of four days a week, and must follow a complex set of strict regulations. They are a picturesque lot, and conversations about their past and present activities make for an entertaining exchange. They will also be delighted to sell you reproductions of paintings, old hand-colored prints, back issues of magazines in excellent condition, and, for the creative and discerning tourist, old postcards to be sent home as unique souvenirs—all at bargain prices.

PLATE 15

RUE DE SEINE

This ancient street, originally a pathway along the ditch leading from the Seine river southward, acquired its name in the fifteenth century.

Located at the heart of the Latin Quarter—Latin because students and masters routinely spoke and wrote in that language until the French Revolution in 1793—the street was famous until the early 1900s for selling produce at bargain prices to the students and workers of the area.

Menpes was not the only artist to be inspired by this unpretentious but venerable street. It also attracted Willy Ronis, the Polish refugee photographer, and Eugène Atget, the French photographer famous for his light-drenched photographs of Paris's empty streets at dawn. The poet Jacques Prévert, who celebrated the everyday and the common folk, wrote a poem entitled "Rue de Seine," describing in a few powerful yet simple words a couple in trouble against the backdrop of an empty nighttime street.

The street has been home to many well-known French characters, including the philanthropic priest Saint Vincent de Paul (Number 1), the poet and critic Charles Baudelaire (Numbers 27 and 57), George Sand, the writer and feminist whose real name was Amandine Aurore Lucile Dupin (Number 31), and even (at Number 25) an imaginary hero—d'Artagnan, the famous swordsman from Alexandre Dumas' classic *The Three Musketeers*.

The working people represented by Menpes have long since been replaced by chic Parisian intellectuals, the spiritual heirs of the Zazous and the Existentialists. Replacing the many small specialty bookstores of yore, dozens of stylish boutiques and upscale delicatessens now cater to their discerning local clientele.

PLATE 16

EARLY MORNING ON THE SEINE

The art historian Kenneth Clark "recognized civilization" in the view from the Pont des Arts.

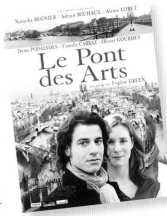

In this early morning scene, before the steamers have appeared on the river, we see the Pont des Arts with the Pont du Carrousel in the distance. Because of its relatively flimsy construction, this pioneering iron bridge was always prone to damage from river traffic, and damage by aerial bombardments in both world wars added to its increasing structural weakness. In 1977 it had to be closed to traffic, and in 1979 a 200-foot section collapsed after a barge rammed into it.

The present bridge was built between 1981 and 1984; the architect Louis Arretche worked hard to keep the open feel of the bridge, at the same time reducing the number of arches from nine to seven to ease river navigation, and realigning the new structure with the Pont Neuf. True to its name, the bridge still serves as a venue for plein air art exhibitions, and many painters, artists, and photographers are drawn to its unique vantage point. It has also starred in a number of films, including its namesake, a French love story starring Natacha Régnier and Denis Podalydès. This 2004 film is set in 1979 and 1980, the dying years of the old iron bridge. The Pont des Arts also features in the last episode of *Sex and the City*.

Kenneth Clark made the statement about civilization in his 1969 study of the same name. "I am standing on the Pont des Arts in Paris," he wrote. "On the one side of the Seine is the harmonious, reasonable facade of the Institute of France, built as a college in about 1670. On the other bank is the Louvre, built continuously from the Middle Ages to the nineteenth century: classical architecture at its most splendid and assured. Just visible upstream is the Cathedral of Notre Dame—not perhaps the most lovable of cathedrals, but the most rigorously intellectual facade in the whole of Gothic art. What is civilization? I do not know. I cannot define it in abstract terms. But I think I can recognize it when I see it—and I am looking at it now."

PLATE 17

AFTERNOON

The old Pont du Carrousel was one of Menpes's favorite places to set up his easel.

This sunset view in delicate pink and orange hues forms a poetic background to the high dome of the Institut de France, home to five French Académies, those characteristically French institutions devoted to promoting French science and culture. The best known, the Académie Française, was founded by Cardinal Richelieu in 1635 under Louis XIII to maintain the standards of purity of the French language, defining the rules of grammar and publishing an official French dictionary.

The "Forty," or the "Immortals," as its members are called, are elected and approved by the French head of state. It was one of the last bastions of male dominance in French academia, the first female "Immortal," Marguerite Yourcenar, being elected in 1980.

Next to the Institut de France is the famous École Nationale des Beaux Arts de Paris, initially a monastery that closed in 1791 to be replaced by a Museum of French Monuments. In 1816 the museum closed its doors and was transformed into the School of Fine Arts.

Numerous French painters have had the honor of being rejected by this august institution, including Paul Cézanne—the reason given being his "excessive temperament." How many of those students, fortunate enough to be awarded a *diplôme*, found themselves raised to the status of Immortal forty or fifty years later?

PLATE 18

NOTRE DAME FROM THE RIVER

A sunset view of the cathedral of Our Lady of Paris, seen from the once peaceful Île Saint-Louis.

Menpes probably set up his easel on the island's Quai d'Orléans to make this painting of the church in delicate tones of blue, purple, and gray. This island, located just behind the larger Île de la Cité, is one of Paris's most subtly seductive areas, with its classical seventeenth-century architecture and small, intimate streets of old-world charm. During the reign of Louis XIII, two small islands were joined and two stone bridges constructed to link the new island to the rest of Paris. The beautifully proportioned facades, wrought-iron balconies, and immense paneled wooden doors hide enchanting inner courtyards and peaceful, spacious apartments with romantic views onto the river.

The Pont Saint Louis leads to the Square Jean XXIII on the Île de la Cité, which replaced the chapels and houses that blocked the magnificent view of Notre Dame and its flying buttresses at the beginning of the nineteenth century. Many poorer Parisians on a relaxing trip down the Seine could thus enjoy the view as they returned from a day out on the river.

Today's visitor to the Île Saint Louis must include a pilgrimage to that famous Paris institution Glaces Berthillon, a shop specializing in handmade ice cream and sherberts in more than seventy flavors, including the unlikely sounding foie gras.

PLATE 19

EARLY MORNING ON THE SEINE

Early riser Menpes has captured an unusual pink and green river symphony
with the Pont d'Austerlitz in the distance.

This bridge was originally built to link the Faubourg Saint-Antoine on the Right Bank to the Jardin des Plantes on the Left Bank. The bridge in the painting was completed in 1885 and was named after the famous battle of Austerlitz, which Napoléon won against the Russians in 1805. Its imperial origins are reflected in a splendid sculpture of a roaring lion holding the Austerlitz flag in its paws.

The Jardin des Plantes—the city's botanic gardens—then, as now, were home to more than 4,500 plant species, an Alpine garden, and several museums, including remarkable collections of dinosaur fossils and huge crystals. The greenhouses that inspired many late nineteenth- and early twentieth-century artists still stand. These remarkable glass and steel structures in the Art Nouveau style house many exotic jungle plants—Douanier

Rousseau, the Naïve artist who painted tropical scenes in a deceptively simple yet technically masterful style, took much of his inspiration from their luxuriant display.

The Jardin also includes a menagerie, one of the oldest zoos in the world, created in 1795 to house the royal menagerie of Versailles. The poets Charles Baudelaire and Rainer Maria Rilke, and the romantic painter Eugène Delacroix, drew artistic inspiration from the big cats in their small enclosures, though you will not see these creatures here today—starting in 1970 the large mammals were moved into more spacious quarters at the Vincennes Zoo.

TOUT PARIS

LE JARDIN DES PLANTES

EN CARTES POSTALES ARTISTIQUES

par

K. F. éditeurs PARIS

PARIS KF ÉDITEURS PARIS

20 CARTES

AU BON MARCHÉ 1.35

1re SÉRIE

Bords de la Seine
Le Port Mazas et le Pont d'Austerlitz
(XIIe et Ve arrts)

Madeleine

Collection F. Fleury

L'ancien Muséum avec les Baleines

Le Jardin des Plantes

PLATE 20

PONT CONCORDE

Menpes's misnamed painting actually depicts the Pont du Carrousel,
and offers a glimpse of the Gare d'Orsay under its arches in the distance.

The huge Gare and Hôtel d'Orsay were erected for the world Exposition of 1900, which attracted more than fifty million visitors to the city. The architect, Victor Laloux, used 12,000 tons of iron (compared with the 7,500 tons used for the Eiffel Tower) to build his daring glass and metal domed roof, then camouflaged the structure with sumptuously carved stone.

Until 1939 the Gare d'Orsay was the mainline terminus for the trains to southwestern France, by which time the station's short platforms had become unsuitable for long-distance trains. Suburban services continued to use it until 1973, when it closed as a station, and in 1977 the building was refurbished as a museum. It is now famous for its collection of nineteenth-century paintings, many by the French Impressionists.

The Gare d'Orsay was not the only remarkable innovation introduced at the 1900 Exposition. The first subway, familiarly known as the métro, was built to link the western and eastern extremities of Paris. It conveyed the crowds to the fair in electrically driven trains; once there they could see showings of early films by the Lumière brothers, and fly through the air in the 328-foot-tall Ferris wheel.

Intérieur de la Gare d'Orsay - C. M.

PARIS. - Intérieur de la Gare d'Orléans, Quai d'Orsay. - Edition E. L., Paris.

88. PARIS
La Grande Roue
C. M.

PLATE 21

THE SEINE NEAR CHARENTON

Menpes has painted a superb view of the town hall of Charenton,
an area that appears to have held a special fascination for him.

He was not alone in his appreciation of this bustling Paris suburb. More than a century earlier, in 1782, the painter Jean-Honoré Fragonard had bought a house in Charenton. Fragonard was one of the premier Rococo artists of his time, famous for his vigorous brushwork. He began studying when he was just fourteen with François Boucher, the colorist master of pinks and blues, many of whose famous pastorals were inspired by the then lush landscapes of Charenton. Later, in the late nineteenth and early twentieth centuries, Charenton attracted hundreds of working families to service the many factories springing up in the area.

The town hall, formerly known as the Pavillon Antoine de Navarre, is an excellent example of early seventeenth-century French architecture, inspired by Italian Baroque but in a more restrained spirit and with steeply pitched roofs. The factory chimney and barges remind us that in Menpes's time the town was an important part of the river economy. What appears to be a large quantity of timber has perhaps just been unloaded from one of the barges anchored along the banks of the Seine.

PLATE 22

FROM BERCY

River transport was a cheap and convenient method for transporting goods, especially wine, to Paris.

During the nineteenth century, Bercy, next to neighboring Charenton, became France's most important transshipment point for French wine, thanks both to its location and to the absence of taxes outside the city limits of Paris. The wine was brought to Bercy by boat in barrels, then unloaded and bottled before being sent off to Parisian restaurants and shops. By 1880 the wine storehouses and warehouses of Bercy were so numerous that they were officially declared as being essential to the city; they continued in use until the mid-twentieth century. Today they have been preserved, and their architecture has inspired Bercy Village, a chic shopping area.

The riverboats, or *péniches*, depicted by Menpes advancing from Bercy down the Seine, were long, deep vessels with living quarters at the stern. They played a crucial role in conveying coal from northern France to Paris. A complex network of canals and locks allowed boats to drop gradually to the Seine from the higher areas north of the city.

Today one of the more fascinating tourist attractions is a 2.8-mile voyage from the Canal Saint Martin in northern Paris to the Port de l'Arsenal near the Bastille. It includes a trip through an underground canal lit by round openings, which have been chosen by the Japanese artist Keichi Tahara as the site of *Echoes of Light*, an intriguing piece of installation art.

368. - PARIS. - Le Canal St-Martin et la Colonne de Juillet

PLATE 23

IN THE MARKET

Paris's markets create a village atmosphere where people can shop and meet their neighbors.

The city's markets can be documented at least as far back as the fifth century. Paris was then called Lutetia, and was centered on what we now know as the Île de la Cité. The first market, called Palu, had the dual function of produce selling, and, like the Athenian agora, providing a place for public debate and pronouncement. By 1860, fifty-one markets were functioning in the city, and today there are more than ninety markets scattered throughout Paris.

Markets then, as now, sold a wide variety of goods—fruit and vegetables, meat, fish, fowl, dairy produce, flowers, household utensils, clothes, and just about anything else you can think of. In the early 1900s, many of the merchants were women, as portrayed here. Each day they would go to the great Halles Centrales to buy the goods they would then hawk from their stands. Unfortunately, these women were often distrusted by the police, who—usually wrongly—suspected them of selling not just food but also themselves.

Some of the attractive stone-built covered markets that Paris is famous for were built to give the authorities more control over the activities of the market women. Today the market business is often a family affair, continued from generation to generation.

880   SCÈNES PARISIENNES. — *Marchande des Quatre-Saisons*   ND Phot

PLATE 24

DÉJEUNER AL FRESCO

Menpes's colorful scene depicts one of the less attractive aspects of Paris in the 1900s.

The vast majority of Parisian workers, especially those who plied their trades and sold their wares in the streets of the city, earned very little and had no retirement or health benefits. Among the least fortunate were the women who sold hot food to their fellows throughout the day. Here we see a group having lunch al fresco (in the cold), sipping hot soup, or—if they were lucky—stew, served by the woman in red with her back to us.

The *marchande de café* with her open-air coffee stand was a common figure in Paris, especially in the area surrounding the market called Les Halles. Maids and restauranteurs would come to Les Halles to purchase produce in the cold, early hours of the morning, and the coffee woman with her urn and coal-burning brazier served café au lait—hot milk and coffee in large bowls—along with rolls.

The composer Gustave Charpentier, a baker's son who entered the Paris Conservatoire in 1881, found much of his inspiration among the working folk of Paris. His opera *Louise*, first performed in 1900, was attended by many working-class people who knew of, and appreciated, the composer's efforts on their behalf. The opera includes the famous line, "Workers want to be bourgeois, the bourgeois want to be aristocrats, aristocrats want to be artists, and artists want to be God." In 1902 Charpentier founded the Conservatoire Populaire Mimi Pinson, established to provide a free artistic education for the city's working girls.

La soupe aux Halles

THÉATRE NATIONAL DE L'OPÉRA COMIQUE

LOUISE
roman musical en 4 actes et 5 tableaux
de Gustave Charpentier

PLATE 25

A FLOWER MARKET

The flower market at the Quai aux Fleurs runs all along the northern edge of the Île de la Cité.

Menpes has painted the women guarding their wares in the sun as the Seine flows by beneath the parapet. They are part of a tradition that in Menpes's time was already a hundred years old, as the Quai aux Fleurs had been created in 1808. During the week the flower sellers offered a wide variety of potted plants and bouquets for Parisians to buy, and even the humblest households usually could afford a box to hang on their balcony to add a note of color.

The art of the bouquet was highly developed, and the market women vied in creating the most attractive bouquets. On Sundays they had a holiday when the Marché aux Oiseaux, the bird market with its thousands of caged birds and the occasional ferret, invaded the banks of the Seine. Fascinating varieties of canaries and finches, with their wonderful colors and ever-varying songs, still tempt visitors today.

One of the fascinations of the flower market was its seasonal variation. Each season brought new species of plants and flowers, some being shipped from distant countries. Spring brought slipper flowers from Chile and heathers from the Cape of Good Hope. In the summer, dahlias, myrtle, and jasmine predominated, while in the autumn it was the many varieties of chrysanthemum held pride of place. Even in the winter many flowers continued to bloom in the greenhouses of southern France and find their way to the market. Pride of place, as in Menpes's painting, was given to the glowing beauty of the rose.

Quai aux fleurs

Le Petit Parisien
Supplément Littéraire Illustré
CINQ CENTIMES

LA FÊTE DU CHRYSANTHÈME
...ficielle du chrysanthème. — Le chrysanthème dans la rue

PLATE 26

AN ORANGE VENDOR

Menpes was always sensitive to the dignity of the hardworking people of the streets.

Here Menpes depicts a street vendor of oranges, with his basket slung over his arm, against the background of an open-air stall selling potatoes. People sold just about anything in the streets, from fruits and vegetables to baskets, knives, and soap. We are extremely fortunate that Eugène Atget, the great French photographer, took many photographs of the open-air vendors in the famous series he began in 1897, without which much of ancient Paris would have disappeared without a trace.

Dismayed by the modernization of the city, Atget set out to capture the disappearing urban landscape of old Paris, including portraits of many of the people who made their living in the street. He identified these street vendors as important remnants of preindustrial France, and had a talent for persuading them to pose with their merchandise.

Interestingly, he included a photograph of his own studio in his *Metiers, Boutiques et Étalages de Paris*, clearly identifying himself as a tradesperson rather than as an artist. His work helped to transform the vision of urban photography, paying attention to the ordinary, the ephemeral, and the poignant rather than concentrating on the posed and the monumental. The American artist Man Ray discovered Atget's photographs in the mid-1920s, and after Atget's death in 1927, Ray's student Berenice Abbott took the bulk of his prints and negatives to the United States, where they now form the Abbott-Levey Collection in New York's Museum of Modern Art.

PLATE 17

RUE DE LA FAYETTE

Then, as now, shopping was an essential element of the Paris experience.

Paris did not have to wait for haute couture to become a city of fashion victims. In 1909 the first *grands magasins*, or department stores, had recently opened in Rue de la Fayette, in the city's Jewish district. In 1893 Théophile Bader and his cousin Alphonse Kahn had opened a fashion store in a small haberdasher's shop at the corner of Rue de la Fayette and Rue de la Chaussée-d'Antin. In 1896 the company purchased the entire building at Number 1 Rue de la Fayette, and in 1905 expanded into the current premises. Women from all over Paris flocked to the new Galeries Lafayette, the "showcase of desire," as it was christened by Émile Zola in his novel *Au Bonheur des Dames*.

The most popular accessories of the period were umbrellas and especially hats. Women still covered themselves with lace and colorful fabrics, though their outlines were noticeably slimmer than twenty years previously. The crinoline had disappeared, but corsets were still much in use, the most fashionable look being a slender S-shape.

The Rue de la Fayette was also home to an open-air market. Nearby were the gigantic Halles, the old wholesale market of the city—"Paris's stomach," as it was affectionately called. The densely populated quarters of the Grands Boulevards and the Opéra made the Rue de la Fayette an excellent place for market gardeners to sell their produce. Fruit and vegetable carts were still pulled mostly by men and oxen, causing many accidents when automobiles first appeared on the scene.

LES PETITS METIERS DE PARIS
Une Marchande des Quatre-Saisons

PLATE 28

MARCHANDES AMBULANTES

Taking time to stroll, choose, and chat was the reward for financial success.

It's a lovely day, and men and women in hats—and therefore probably from one of the wealthier neighborhoods of the capital—are strolling leisurely, with no real destination in view. They stop to admire the fruits and vegetables sold by the street vendors who have come into the city from the surrounding countryside to sell their products at decent prices to the bourgeoisie.

In the distance we can just distinguish a café with "Distillerie" written above its awning, where shoppers could order a glass of the celebrated absinthe, the wormwood-based liquor that was still legal in 1909 but was to be banned throughout France in 1915. The vivid green concoction contributed much to the mythology of poets such as Paul Verlaine but also ravaged the population, as described by the French realist novelist Émile Zola in his famous novel *L'Assommoir* (*The Drunkard*).

This street scene includes a profusion of flags and advertising messages. Until the end of the nineteenth century, there was no legislation to stop anyone from painting large advertisements on their walls. In one photograph taken by the well-known French photographer Eugène Atget, a large wall-painted advertisement for "Cola Kocca" is clearly visible. In 1899, however, a new law was passed and everything changed. Soon the famous "Défense d'afficher" (stick no bills) stencil started to appear on walls throughout the capital.

2130. PARIS — La première femme, colleuse d'affiches

PLATE 29

RAG PICKER

In the Paris of 1900, *les pauvres*, the poor, or *les miséreux*, the miserable people, were legion.

Those at the bottom of the income ladder, such as the ragpicker portrayed here, earned their living by practicing humble trades. Menpes paints a portrait of a hardworking woman, poorly dressed, seated with her few small treasures on one of the stone benches that line the banks of the Seine. She is examining the results of her quest through the streets of Paris for old clothes thrown away by their previous owners.

Parisians with a secure livelihood had an enormous ambivalence in relation to *les pauvres*. These people, living on the margin, were seen as the "salt of the earth" who did well not to descend to criminality and begging. Yet the relationship of the secure with the insecure was thoroughly imbued with paternalism and moral superiority. *Les pauvres* were people to be criticized, pitied, and "saved."

Destitute women like the ragpicker Menpes has portrayed with sensitivity and compassion often became what a 1900 pamphlet writer refers to as "poor abandoned girls, widows, or deserted women, and nannies who have become pregnant," what Jeremy Bentham, the nineteenth-century British reformer and philosopher, termed "imperfect workers." Is our ragpicker destined to become one of these? Is she perhaps one already? We cannot tell from the painting, but Menpes, in his sympathy for the Parisian underclass, has painted a stark portrait of the social realities of the early twentieth century.

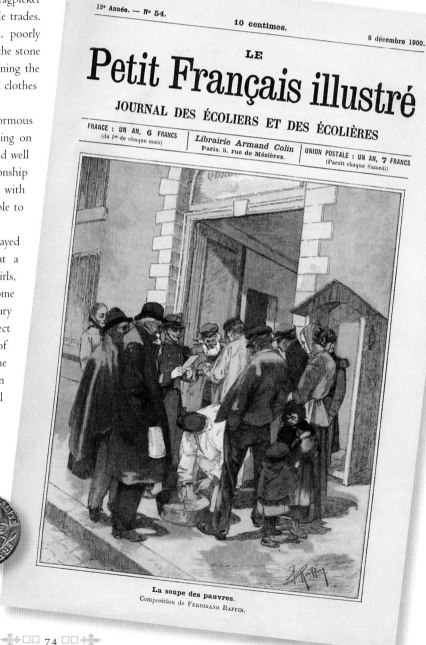

La soupe des pauvres.
Composition de FERDINAND RAFFIN.

PLATE 30

FACTORY CHIMNEYS

Joinville le Pont at Charenton was one of the newly industrial areas that Menpes often painted.

Like so many factories in an age that still depended on river transportation, this one is located on the banks of the Seine. In front of the factories we can just make out a steamer, or at least the smoke rising from its chimney. Compared with more heavily industrialized countries like Britain and the United States, France was lagging somewhat behind in industrial development. In 1909, for example, there were just 3,000 steam vessels in France compared with 15,000 in Great Britain.

France's industrial revolution started considerably later than England's, one result being that the legal framework embracing corporate and social life in the two countries differs noticeably. Strongly influenced by the philosophers of the Age of Enlightenment, France was—and still is—a society that is relatively ill at ease with the free-market philosophy of the English-speaking world, being used to a more socially responsible, centrally planned, and protectionist concept of industrial development.

None of this, however, is evident in the painting, where the landscape is gloomy and desolate in spite of the beauty of the color harmonies of violet and sap green. It presents rather a sad vision of the world of the factory workers.

PLATE 31

ON THE WAY TO CHARENTON

Menpes painted Charenton so many times we must imagine
that he lived here while making the paintings for the 1909 book.

Charenton-le-Pont is located in a strategic location near the city of Paris next to one of the oldest bridges spanning the Seine. The bridge—*pont*—included in its name was first mentioned in the histories during the seventh century. For such a small town it played an important part in the Hundred Years War with the English, finally concluded in 1453, and more recently in the war against Bismarck in 1870 that led to the fall of the Second Empire. It was also the site of a famous asylum for the mentally ill, where the Marquis de Sade was imprisoned from 1803 until his death in 1814.

By 1900 Charenton had become a "new city," as is evident from the painting. The town's many factories were staffed by workers from the rural exodus. Located not far from Paris, but less expensive and without the city's restrictive laws and taxes, Charenton underwent considerable urban development during this period, with entire districts being completely rebuilt.

An important reason why Menpes painted Charenton and its environs so many times stems from the influence of James McNeill Whistler, the Massachusetts-born Impressionist and Menpes's teacher and mentor. Like many of the French Impressionists of the period, Whistler found the novel patterns, colors, and atmospheric effects of industrial areas fascinating to paint.

159. CHARENTON — Le Pont
Embarcadère des bateaux Parisiens

PLATE 32

NEAR CHARENTON

As we approach Charenton, a landscape of factories and their tall chimneys emerges in the distance.

The first decades of the nineteenth century brought the beginnings of industrialization to Charenton. The 1850s saw the development of a metalworking factory called La Fonderie Anglaise alongside the road to Paris, while the main Paris-Lyon railway, opened in 1849, involved the demolition of Charenton's only important ancient buildings, belonging to a Carmelite convent.

The last decades of the nineteenth century saw Charenton's population boom. In 1856 it had been a village of just 4,500 people; by 1909 it had exceeded 20,000. The greatest period of growth followed the complete reconstruction of the bridge between 1861 and 1863, accompanied by the development of three substantial port areas at Saint-Maurice, Carrières, and Magasins Généraux.

This area east of Paris is still generally poorer today than the city's western suburbs, though in recent years it has received much investment and is becoming a popular area with young professionals. Because the Parisian police had no jurisdiction over this area until 1941, it had its own laws, which were much more lenient. In Charenton you could drink as much as you liked and party all night.

PLATE 33

DRYING GROUND NEAR CHARENTON

Freshly washed laundry dries in the open air at the water's edge along the banks of the Seine.

Many women worked to keep the city's linen clean and aired. The items drying here are perhaps the tablecloths and sheets from some of the many new suburban houses being built in Charenton at that time, but they may also have come from one of the restaurants serving the neighboring Vincennes fairgrounds, or the Vélodrome, which in 1900 had played host to the Olympic Games.

When a Paris venue for the second modern Olympic Games was decided on, the first having taken place in Greece in 1896, the Parisian populace had absolutely no interest in Pierre de Coubertin's desire to maintain the ancient Greek sporting tradition. But when the city decided to develop the eastern part of Paris by building the first electric streetcar and subway lines,

excitement began to build. These were the games that saw the British tennis player, Charlotte Cooper, become the first woman ever to win an Olympic medal.

The Bois de Vincennes was also renowned for its many fairs, such as the Fête du Trône, which brought carnival people together in the largest fairground of the era. There were shooting ranges, fortune-tellers, and merry-go-rounds for the pleasure of families that came for a Sunday outing. Sometimes children returned on a Thursday afternoon to enjoy the rides again. The Bois de Vincennes was also the site of one of the first movie studios, built by Charles Pathé in 1896.

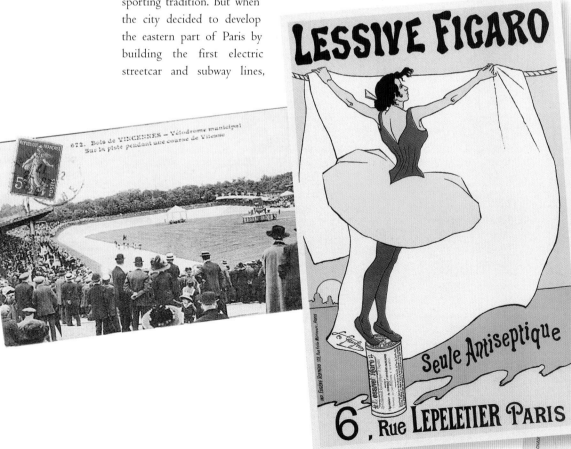

PLATE 34

A STROLL ON THE BOULEVARD

Anyone visiting Paris in 1909 who had last been in the city three decades earlier would hardly have recognized it.

Between 1871 and 1914 the population of Paris grew by leaps and bounds, from 1.8 million inhabitants to almost three million. As a result the city changed dramatically, and perhaps the most dramatic change of all was the creation of Haussmann's wide boulevards—Les Grands Boulevards. These new spaces offered new ways of selling, which combined the old ways of the street vendors with the new ways of advertising and stacked displays, though the man with his pipe in Menpes's painting appears completely indifferent to the wares on sale.

The boulevards brought automobiles to the city's streets, and hosted the first moving picture shows, made by the Lumière brothers. These were shown in small tents where people paid one sou to experience the seventh art. The first subway stations appeared in the boulevards too, their entrances designed by Hector Guimard in the fashion known as *style nouille*, or "noodle style," descriptive of their organic forms.

Buildings around the Grands Boulevards—in the Place de la Bourse and the Rue Réaumur—now started to rise higher thanks to the invention of the elevator and a new law that allowed architects to design buildings up to seven stories high. But our strolling man does not look upward. Unlike New York, Paris is to be appreciated not for the soaring height of its buildings but for being in contact with its streets, its small shops, its street vendors, and its endless parade of Parisian men, women, and children.

Plate 35

PEELING POTATOES

In the first decade of the twentieth century, groups of itinerant workers could be found on every corner.

The city's streets were the workplace for many poorer Parisians—the coal men, the grinders sharpening knives, the salt carriers, and the women sitting on their stools with a hot water bottle on their knees selling *petits noirs*—little black cups of coffee—for a sou to workers on their way to the factory. Then there were the political agitators, trying to avoid being caught by the police as they sold their illegally printed pamphlets, and the goatherds who brought their capricious goats down from Montmartre to sell their milk at a higher price than they could get for it in the countryside.

The potato peelers, like those painted by Menpes, would bring their vegetables to the city streets to prepare them, and sell them to maids and cooks from the wealthier houses.

Menpes's potato peelers include some older women—the first French law on retirement, which became law in 1898, applied only to workers in the subway system. By 1909 there were laws governing retirement for factory and rural workers, but these were poorly understood and rarely enforced. Many poorer women, like these in Menpes's painting, worked until they were too old or too infirm to continue.

PLATE 36

IN THE RUE ST. HONORÉ

This well-known Paris street is famous today, as it was
a hundred years ago, for its elegant town houses and luxury boutiques.

The street's most notable landmark, the Élysée Palace at Number 55, was originally built in 1722 for Louis Henri de La Tour d'Auvergne, the Count d'Evreux. In those days the street was a path running parallel to the Champs Élysées, then just a large garden. When the Count d'Evreux died, Louis XV purchased the palace as a gift for his celebrated mistress, the Marquise de Pompadour.

During the second half of the eighteenth century, wealthy financiers began to build luxurious town houses, or *hôtels particuliers*, along the Champs Élysées, and the d'Evreux Palace took the name of the adjacent avenue. After Madame de Pompadour died, the building changed hands several times. In 1816 Napoléon Bonaparte purchased the Élysée Palace, and during the Second Republic the *députés*—the members of the French parliament—offered it to the president to use as an official residence.

The Champs Élysées became the place for high society to gather and promenade, followed by dinner at Ledoyen, as described by the writer Marcel Proust. Luxury stores sprung up along the Rue Saint-Honoré, such as Maison Hermes,

which opened at Number 24 in 1879. The boutiques were joined by embassies and luxurious town houses, such as the legendary Palais Rose, built in 1896 by the aristocrat Boni de Castellane, who gave huge parties there three times a week. As many as two thousand guests would be invited, their cars lining up all the way to the Place de l'Étoile. What we see in Menpes's picture, however, is not the more upscale side of the street but its opening onto the Rue de Rivoli. Behind its arches are small shops and hurrying shoppers—maybe desperate to find a *tenue*, or outfit, for tonight's party.

PLATE 37

PONT DE L'ALMA

Named after a Crimean War victory, the Pont de l'Alma is now also
famous as the site of the underpass where Diana, Princess of Wales, died in 1997.

The original bridge was named after the Battle of Alma where
in 1854 a coalition army composed of French, English, Turkish,
and Piedmontese soldiers defeated the Russians in Crimea. It
was completed in 1856, and this is the bridge we see in Menpes's
painting. In 1974 the original bridge was replaced, because of the
need for a wider bridge to accommodate Paris's modern traffic.

In this picture, Mortimer Menpes paints a bridge whose
arches are almost completely covered by a flooding Seine. This
is particularly interesting because one of the Pont de l'Alma's
major claims to fame is its famous "Zouave" statue, representing
a soldier from the Battle of Alma. The name Zouave derives from
the Zouaouas, Algerian soldiers who fought alongside the French
army in the Crimea, and the sculpture is used by Parisians to check
on the level of the Seine. When the river rises to cover the Zouave's
feet, the riverbank streets are closed to traffic. In 1910, during the
Seine's highest-ever floods, the river reached his shoulders.

A monument called the Flame of the Pont de l'Alma was given
to Paris in 1987 by the *International Herald Tribune* to commemorate
the friendship between the United States and France; since 1997
it has also been adopted by Diana's admirers as a place to honor
her memory.

PLATE 38

FRUIT AND FLOWERS

In the Paris streets of the 1900s, the day was punctuated
by the various activities of its workingwomen.

The bread and milk carriers were the first to appear on the streets, going from door to door before six o'clock in the morning. Then the washerwomen would appear; they not only washed your clothes but ironed them as well. These women were better paid than most, because they had to be apprenticed for two years to learn their job before being allowed to work for the statutory two francs a day.

Later in the morning you would see a bevy of young girls in their teens, carrying dresses from shops to apartments, or beautiful bouquets from flower markets to the great town houses and luxurious palaces.

By midday the fruit and flower sellers portrayed here would have set up their stands, protecting their products from the sun with huge umbrellas. Humbler than the shopkeepers, they were just as much a part of the city scene as they stood near their baskets and carts, talking loudly in the old Parisian accent, waiting for passersby to stop and admire their products.

These women would have been up since the crack of dawn, bargaining for their products at Les Halles, Paris's central market, and though they each had their favorite corners, they had to be constantly on the move. They were not allowed to stand for long in one place, on pain of being arrested by the police for obstruction and harassment.

PLATE 39

SHOP NEAR CENTRAL MARKET

The central market was more usually called Les Halles, a name still used today even though a huge mall has taken its place.

The biggest market in Paris, Les Halles was first built in 1183 and was soon given the nickname "the stomach of Paris." It was rebuilt in 1543 under François I, and most comprehensively in 1870 by the famous architect Victor Baltard. The massive steel and glass "Pavillon Baltard," officially named the Halle Saint-Pierre, was so impressive and innovative that even Victor Hugo wrote about it. In 1986 the structure became home to a cultural center that houses, among other things, a Museum of Naïve Art and a performing venue.

Les Halles always posed something of a problem. The huge market was difficult to control, hard for the police and city authorities to supervise, not always respectful of hygiene, and peopled by odd and suspicious characters. Yet the city could not have survived without it, since the bulk of the ordinary Parisians' diet passed through the great market.

Little of this is apparent in Menpes's painting, since he shows us a scene very early in the morning, when the maids from large houses came to buy the day's necessities from small shops like this one. With her large white apron, the woman in the foreground appears to be a cream seller, washing the utensils after she and her partner have sold all their wares. Now they are getting ready to return to the countryside, leaving the central market to its daytime bustle.

PLATE 40

A FRUIT SELLER

This white-haired old woman has pushed her heavy cart
all the way to Paris to sell her produce on the Grands Boulevards.

She has come from one of the villages surrounding Paris
that specialized in market gardens, now sadly replaced by
industrial areas and housing estates. One such important area
was Clignancourt to the north of the city, today the site of one
of Paris's famous flea markets, or *marché au puces*. Bobigny, along
the banks of the Ourcq canal, is today one of the rare suburbs
of Paris where a number of active farms can still be found, their
proprietors still "going down" to Paris to sell the fruits of their
labor in the outdoor markets.

In 1909 this was not an easy task. In 1896 there had been
a change in the regulations governing Les Halles, the Parisian
central market, after it was discovered that too many small-scale
producers were being exploited, even forced to pay bribes to the
police in order to be allowed to sell their produce. Probably one
of the reasons this elderly person has chosen to sell her products
to passing customers in the street is to avoid the necessity of
paying a "security fee."

PLATE 41

AT THE NEUILLY FLOWER MARKET

Who is this charming girl we see buying flowers?

Perhaps she is a maid sent by a rich family to buy flowers for the house, since she is wearing a dress of a beautiful pink material that matches her hat and shows her legs. Colorful dresses showed that you worked for an upper-class family. Or perhaps she is a young woman home from boarding school, spending a weekend with her parents in their villa in Neuilly, a favorite country retreat.

The name Neuilly comes from *noue*, a marshy valley, and *lun*, or forest—Neuilly lies between the Seine and the Bois de Boulogne. It started life as a small harbor on the Seine, where the monks ran a ferry service. In 1900 Neuilly was still the countryside and not the wealthy Parisian suburb it is today. Many people from high society had a house there, though others, such as the Count of Monte Cristo in Alexandre Dumas' famous novel, preferred

the more rural Auteuil. Neuilly was close to the city and so convenient, and yet people could feel they were in the country.

During the belle epoque, more and more Parisians bought houses or pieces of land to build on in Neuilly. Little by little, the countryside evolved into a leafy suburb, characterized by broad avenues lined with huge trees, and charming, secluded residences hidden among trees and shrubs.

Today the suburb of Neuilly-sur-Seine, whose former mayor, Nicolas Sarkozy, became president of France in 2007, is *the* place to live for anyone who is anyone in French society.

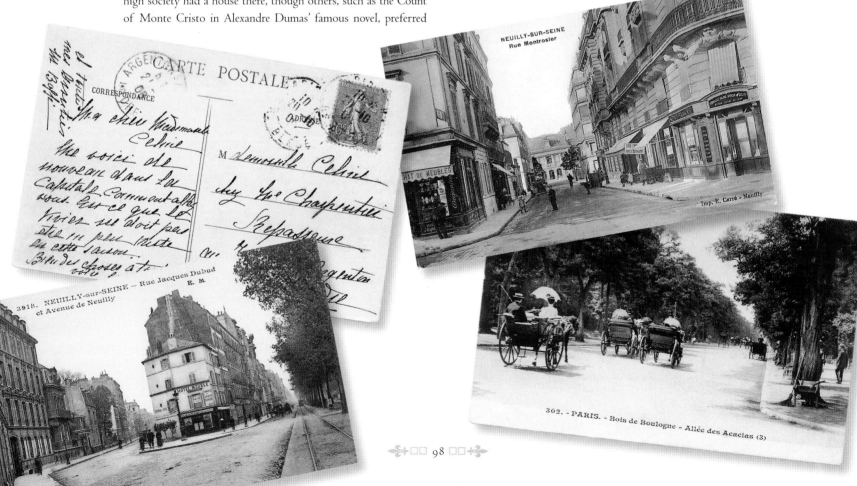

PLATE 42

IN THE TUILERIES

Pierre Bonnard, French Postimpressionist and contemporary of Menpes,
often painted charming scenes of children playing in the Tuileries gardens.

Menpes here records the common scene of a small boy, dressed in a sailor suit, playing while out with his nanny, or perhaps his aunt.

During the time of Marcel Proust, of tea-and-madeleine fame, the Tuileries Garden that leads from the Louvre to the Place de la Concorde and the Avenue des Champs Élysées was considered more chic than the Luxembourg Garden, while Saint Germain des Prés was considered, by the upper classes, too far from the Champs Élysées for anything of consequence to happen there. As a countess friend of Marcel Proust asked her daughter when she was obliged to move from the Rue Saint-Honoré to Boulevard Saint-Michel, "And when do they harvest the hay over there?"

The Jardin des Tuileries, the oldest French-style garden in Paris, was initially inspired by the sixteenth-century Italian style, with six vertical and eight horizontal alleys dividing it into rectangles. In 1664 André Le Nôtre, creator of the Versailles gardens, added a round pond at each of its entrances, where, then as now, young boys and girls can hire miniature sailing boats to wend their way around the ducks.

The gardens have witnessed many an unusual event, including the first manned air-balloon flight by François Pilâtre de Rozier and the Marquis d'Arlandes, on November 21, 1783.

PLATE 43

PARIS BY NIGHT

"Paris by night" usually evokes a somewhat different scene than this empty street!

Where is the Moulin Rouge? Where are the dancers throwing their legs in the air as they dance the cancan? Where is Sarah Bernhardt, the actress capable of moving her audience to tears night after night? Menpes's painting has nothing to do with any of these nighttime attractions but is rather a simple portrayal of those many rainy November days when Paris looks rather like London.

Like a shadow in the distance stands the Luxembourg Palace, where the Senate now holds its sessions. It was built by Marie de Médicis in 1615 and modeled on the palaces of Florence, her native city. It was where Louis XIV raised his children, and it later became a terrible jail during the Revolution.

In other parts of the City of Light, however, "Paris by night" *was* delivering on its promise. Opened in 1889, Le Moulin Rouge at Pigalle was the center of a whirl of extravagant parties every night. Nicknamed the "women's palace," it had a scandalous reputation, especially for the "Cleopatra Parade," where a naked woman was carried onstage by four men, surrounded by equally unclothed women reclining on flowery beds.

Among the cabaret's most famous dancers was La Goulue, who danced the cancan better than anyone—except perhaps for her friends Jeanne la Folle, "La Môme Fromage" (thus named because she was so young), and "Nini Pattes en l'Air" (Nini Legs in the Air). All these young girls were immortalized in striking pastels and paintings by Henri de Toulouse-Lautrec, famous for the delightful bon mot, "I'll drink milk when cows graze on grapes!"

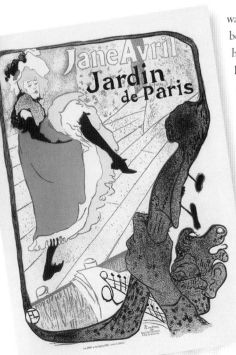

PLATE 44

THE PONT DES ARTS (LATE AFTERNOON)

With his delicate brushwork, Menpes demonstrates how well and truly he has adopted the Impressionist philosophy.

Although strongly influenced by the painting style of the French Impressionists, the American painter James McNeil Whistler founded his own movement, Aestheticism, and his strong personality influenced many English and American artists, including Mortimer Menpes, who studied with him from 1880 onward. Whistler was also a master etcher, and taught the technique to Menpes, who later developed the color etching process he used to illustrate many of his books. In fact, some of the "paintings," primarily the crowd scenes, are in fact etchings.

Considered a precursor to the twentieth-century abstract movement, Whistler believed that a painting should be a beautiful arrangement of colors and forms. The French Impressionists were fascinated by atmospheric, transient effects—hence the name of the movement, derived from the title of Claude Monet's 1873 painting *Impression, Soleil Levant*. Like them, Whistler chose his subjects not for their historical or sentimental importance but for their potential as a formal exercise. His titles, often beginning with "Harmony" or "Arrangement," emphasize his vision of "pure" painting.

In Menpes's *Paris*, the paintings of bridges and factories at dawn and dusk predominate. Clearly he shared his mentor's fascination for atmosphere and for reality as an exercise in abstraction, both evident in this lovely pink, lavender, and pale yellow arrangement of the famous Pont des Arts at dusk.

PLATE 45

A CRÉMERIE IN THE RUE ST. HONORÉ

As Charles de Gaulle liked to say, "How can you possibly govern a country that has 258 different kinds of cheese?"

Did all these cheeses exist in 1900? There were almost certainly even more then than there are today, since many varieties have disappeared with the rise of modern consumer society. As we can see in this painting, a *crémerie* is not just a place where one bought cream—it also sold milk, two churns of which are displayed on the left, directly on the pavement, as well as butter and a wide selection of cheeses.

As for yogurt, it had not yet become the dietary staple that it is today. King Francis I was offered a sample in 1542 by the Turkish sultan, who had learned that the king of France suffered from stomach troubles. It was not until 1910, following studies by Nobel Prize–winner Elie Metchnikoff proving its beneficial effects on babies, that this Bulgarian invention began to spread around the world. As Jean de La Fontaine, the witty and misanthropic seventeenth-century French writer, wrote in his fable *The Fox and the Crow*, "This lesson is doubtless worth a cheese" ("Cette leçon vaut bien un fromage, sans doute").

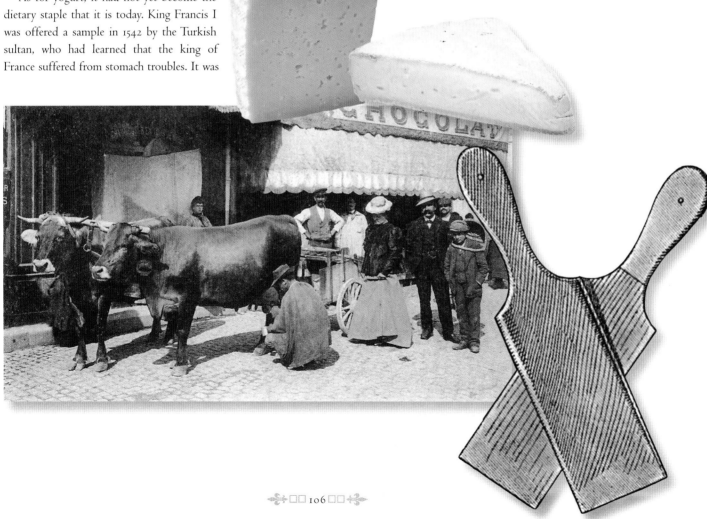

PLATE 46

PONT DE TOURNELLE

Here is a view you will never see again—the bridge, whose name was actually Pont de la Tournelle, no longer exists.

Built in 1656, this famous bridge was so damaged during the 1910 floods that it had to be demolished. The current of the Seine is extremely strong at the tip of the Île Saint-Louis, where the bridge was located, and the first Pont de la Tournelle, built in 1340 above the old medieval fort that once defended Paris, was similarly destroyed by floodwaters.

In this painting, Menpes shows us Notre Dame from the back; on the right is the Île Saint-Louis. By this time, Île de la Cité, the cradle of Lutetia (the Roman name for the town that grew to become Paris), had already been completely transformed by Baron Haussmann and Napoléon III. Except for Notre Dame and the beautiful Chapelle Saint-Louis, now hidden inside the Palais de Justice, the narrow, winding streets of the island were almost completely eliminated to make room for official government buildings, including the headquarters of the city police, the city courthouse, and the *tribunal de commerce*, the court that specialized in trade disputes. In this way the government took steps to ensure that no new revolution, or even the early stages of a minor rebellion, could begin in the Île de la Cité.

The only turmoil you will see today is the turbulent motion of the river, no longer a threat to the strong new bridge built in 1924. The bridge is protected by a statue of Saint Geneviève, the city's patron saint, who, in 451 at the age of twenty-eight, led the people of Paris in their defeat of the barbarian invaders.

4035. PARIS – Pont des Tournelles

PLATE 47

THE LOUVRE

The Louvre is the largest museum in the world; this is the view from the banks of the Seine.

The Louvre, former castle of the French monarchy, covers a total of 525,282 square feet. Behind the arches and hidden from our eyes is the equestrian statue of Louis XIV. The Sun King spent a sad childhood here, in what was then an enormous and barely heated castle, built in 1190 by King Philippe Auguste. He was threatened on several occasions by the *fronde*, an aristocratic revolt. Once he had been crowned king, he decided to build his own chateau at Versailles, where from 1678 he ruled as absolute monarch.

Even when it was still a castle and not yet a museum, the Louvre housed a world-famous collection of paintings. Artists were invited to view the galleries and copy paintings to learn their art. The Louvre was transformed into a museum only after

the Revolution of 1789—in 1791 the revolutionary Assemblée Nationale decreed that the "Louvre and the Tuileries together will be a national palace to house the king and for gathering together all the monuments of the sciences and the arts." The Muséum Central des Arts opened its doors on August 10, 1793. Under the authority of the minister of the interior, its first governors were the painters Hubert Robert and Jean-Honoré Fragonard, the sculptor Augustin Pajou, and the architect Charles de Wailly.

Admission was free, with artists given priority over the general public, who were admitted only on weekends. The works, mostly paintings from the collections of the French royal family and aristocrats who had fled abroad, were displayed in the Salon Carré and the Grande Galerie.

PLATE 48

SHOP BY THE SIDE OF THE SEINE

What are these women looking at—provisions to fill their capacious baskets?

Given their dress, the women are almost certainly maids. They have probably just left their *chambres de bonne*, or maid's rooms, at the top of the Haussmann-style buildings, gone down to the second or the third floor, the "noble floors," to ask their employers what they would like to have for lunch, and then gone off to the banks of the Seine, where innumerable products were delivered daily by boat and sold by small grocery shops or street vendors.

Though they are not wearing the typical *coiffes bretonnes*, or Breton caps, we can imagine that these women come from Brittany, like the well-known little girl Bécassine. Bécassine first appeared in the

girls' magazine *La Semaine de Suzette* in 1905—she was a Breton maid who, at the tender age of ten, left her native Quimper to work, first as a seamstress, then as a waitress, and finally as the maid to La Marquise de Grand Air. Bécassine also was featured in a film of 1939, and Bécassine dolls are still popular in France.

Breton servants were a characteristic part of the population of old Paris. The "sardine crisis" of 1902, when overfishing caused stocks to collapse, forced many young girls from Brittany to leave home and work in Paris. Over 100,000 of them worked as maids, but others became *filles de joie* in brothels such as the famous Chabannais in the Second Arrondissement, with its golden bathroom on the top floor.

PLATE 49

THE PONT DES ARTS

Opened in 1804, this graceful structure was the city's first metal bridge.

Large iron bridges were pioneered in England in the late 1780s; the metal arches of the Pont des Arts, only the third iron bridge to be built anywhere in the world, were Napoléon's proof that his country was in every way equal to its historic rival. Unused to such large open structures, aesthetes wrote disparagingly about it as an unsightly metallic structure, while doctors convinced their patients that walking over it could imperil their health.

A hundred years later, disdain had mutated into a love affair between Parisians and the bridge they still cherish. The bridge's 509 feet, connecting the Institut de France and the Louvre, then known as the Muséum Central des Arts—the origin of the name Pont des Arts—had become one of the most pleasant of Parisian places to wander.

During the belle epoque, orange trees and laurels of the original 1803 glass houses, with their rare plants, were very much a part of the mystique of the bridge, whose initial design included plans for a garden. The bridge became a favorite lovers' trysting place, where one might see a handkerchief dropped by a young girl as a keepsake for her lover. It was also the ideal spot for a passionate midnight assignation, or where a disappointed lover could indulge his grief; indeed, it was a tempting and regularly frequented jumping-off point for suicide attempts.

Jean Renoir, grandson of the painter and a well-known French film director, had his famous character Boudu, a colorful Parisian tramp, jump from the Pont des Arts in his 1932 comic film *Boudu Sauvé des Eaux* (*Boudu Saved from a Watery Death*).

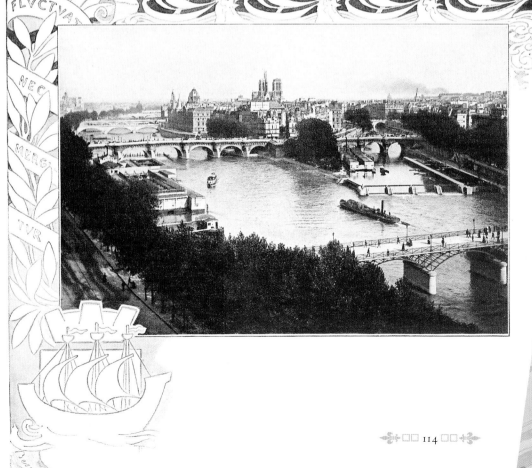

PLATE 50

STEAMERS AT CHARENTON

The Quai de Bercy at Charenton was one of Menpes's favorite subjects.

Other painters of the period, including the early and influential Impressionist Antoine Guillemet, regularly painted the bridge and river at Charenton. Here we can see the steamers and barges moored along the quays, and the steam from the trains bringing goods and passengers into and out of Paris.

Not far from Bercy and Charenton is Paris's Gare de Lyon, a mainline terminus for trains to the south of France opened in 1900 to coincide with the Exposition. Considered a classic example of early twentieth-century architecture, its main feature is a clock tower that echoes the style of the clock tower of the Houses of Parliament in London, home to Big Ben.

In 1901 the Gare de Lyon opened its famous restaurant, the Buffet de la Gare de Lyon, later renamed Le Train Bleu after the legendary Calais-Paris-Riviera express—with its blue-painted sleeping cars—inaugurated in 1922. The restaurant has lost nothing of its magnificence today with its high ceilings, gold-leaf decorations and moldings, chandeliers and fine furniture, as well as forty-one murals representing the destinations of trains served by the station.

Jean Giraudoux, the French dramatist who railed against "modern" monuments such as the Eiffel Tower, wrote, "This place is a museum, but no one realizes it. Time will tell." Indeed it did—in 1972 the restaurant was officially designated a historical monument.

PLATE 51

A CAFÉ CHANTANT

A "café of song," probably located either in the Bois de Vincennes or at the Pavillon d'Ermenonville.

Small restaurants, or *guingettes*, such as this one were a favorite subject of the French Impressionists, particularly Pierre-Auguste Renoir and Claude Monet, who would set up their outdoor easels at La Grenouillère or Au bal du Moulin de la Galette to execute the paintings they are so famous for today. Writers such as Guy de Maupassant and composers such as Georges Bizet also drew inspiration from these establishments.

The *guingettes* along the banks of the Marne to the east of Paris held popular balls for the city's working classes. Because of their location just outside Paris, they were able to avoid taxes on wine and foodstuffs. Restaurants located at the heart of the Bois de Vincennes enjoyed similar success. With the construction of the first railways and streetcars, Parisians found it easy to take a day trip to the area.

To the west of the city, in the Bois de Boulogne, barouches, or coupés, would descend the Avenue de la Grande Armée and pull up in front of premier establishments such as the Pavillon d'Ermenonville or the Chalet des Îles, which was situated on a small artificial island built in the middle of the lake. The clientele of these more formal restaurants did not dance, preferring to dine and gossip with other celebrities on the way back from horse racing at Longchamp or Auteuil, where anyone who was anyone went to be seen.

Whether this painting depicts one of the lighthearted *guingettes* to the east of the city or one of the more upscale restaurants to the west, Menpes's composition of nocturnal festivities tempts us to walk out from under the pine trees and take a seat at one of the tables.

PLATE 52

AT THE NEUILLY FÊTE

Inaugurated in 1815 by the Emperor Napoléon I, the Neu-Neu
has been a favorite of Parisians for almost two hundred years.

Organized in September to prolong that vacation spirit so dear to the hearts of the French, the fair originated as a festival honoring Saint John the Baptist. The name "Neu-Neu" comes from the suburb of Neuilly, where the fair is held, but is also an old French expression meaning "foolish," appropriate for a carnival atmosphere where people can let go and relax.

Jacques Prévert, one of France's most beloved poets, was born in 1900 in Neuilly, both then and now a very chic part of Paris. In spite of his upper-class background, the anarchist poet had a passion for popular forms of art, including the fair he wrote about so often. As a child he may well have visited the stand seen in the picture. The fair was certainly a paradise for children, who often returned home after a long day of cotton candy and waffles with a hint of stomachache.

Maurice Chevalier, the internationally acclaimed French singer, sang "La Fête à Neu-Neu" to celebrate the joys of a day spent eating, drinking, and enjoying the rollercoaster and other attractions with an attractive girl on one's arm. Here even the poorest could forget their troubles and enjoy the music, food, clowns, and rides on the wooden merry-go-round horses.

FÊTE de NEUILLY — American-Aviator

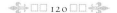

PLATE 53

FÊTE—HÔTEL DES INVALIDES

It is July 14—Bastille Day—and the tricolor flags are out in force.

This scene is set on the Esplanade des Invalides, where the very first Bastille Day celebrations took place in 1790. It is only relatively recently that July 14 became an official national holiday, a decision made during the Third Republic, in 1880.

For many, the July 14 festivities commemorate the fall of the Bastille, a Parisian prison where a few criminals were incarcerated, but which was principally perceived as the very incarnation of the arbitrary powers exercised by the ancien régime. However, the deputies of the National Assembly considered the taking of the Bastille on July 14, 1789, as too violent an event to be celebrated. Officially it is the Feast of the Federation on July 14, 1790, organized to bring all France's provinces to the esplanade of the Champ de Mars near the Invalides Square, that is being commemorated.

The year 1880 was also the year the French adopted *La Marseillaise* as their national anthem. An annual military parade was also initiated at the Hippodrome of Longchamp in the western part of Paris, which today hosts horse racing—the military parade now takes place in the Champs Élysées.

In this late afternoon scene, the parade has long gone past, and so much wine, syrup, and liqueurs have been drunk that the Parisians, replete, have returned home to rest.

PLATE 51

PONT DE SOLFERIENS

Menpes has made a slight mistake in naming the bridge in this painting
Pont de Solferiens—its actual name is the Pont de Solferino.

Like the Pont de la Tournelle, the bridge depicted in this painting no longer exists. It was demolished in 1960, a hundred years after its construction.

First built in 1861 under Napoléon III, the bridge was made of cast iron, and was the first of its kind in Paris. It was baptized Solferino, like so many other bridges in France, after a French military victory. In 1859 the emperor's army defeated the Austrian army at Solferino in Italy. Napoléon was keeping his promise to help Victor Emmanuel II unify Italy, and—incidentally—ensuring that the Savoie and Nice regions would become part of France.

After the demolition of the bridge, the only bridge leading from the Tuileries Garden to the Musée d'Orsay in the heart of Paris was a small, strangely shaped little footbridge. It took another forty years for a replacement to be built, the Passerelle Solferino, designed by the architect Marc Mimram, which was constructed in 1999. It was later renamed Passerelle Léopold Sédar Senghor, to commemorate the famous African poet and president of Senegal. Spanning the Seine in a single arch made predominantly of exotic woods, the new bridge is exclusively reserved for pedestrian use.

PLATE 55

THE OPÉRA

By the time the Opéra opened in 1875, Napoléon III, who had commissioned the building,
had been forced to abdicate and flee to exile in England.

The Palais Garnier is the thirteenth theater to house the Paris Opéra since it was founded by Louis XIV in 1669. It was built on the orders of Napoléon III as part of the great Parisian reconstruction project carried out by Baron Haussmann. The project was put out to competition and won by Charles Garnier, an unknown thirty-five-year-old architect. Building work, which lasted from 1860 to 1875, was interrupted by numerous incidents, including the 1870 war, the fall of the Empire, and the Commune. The Palais Garnier was inaugurated on January 15, 1875.

During the building's inception, Parisians wondered what divine madness had possessed Garnier to build the edifice. In 1867, during the inauguration of the first phase of construction, Empress Eugénie commented to the architect, "It's magnificent, but it is not Louis XIV, or Louis XV, or Louis XVI, so tell me, Monsieur Garnier, what style is it?" The architect proudly replied, "This is the style of Napoléon the Third, Your Majesty."

The building was inspired by St. Peter's Basilica in Rome, and designed to be rigorously symmetrical. The stairs, especially the magnificent main staircase, were widely admired for the use of different colored marble. Garnier, a modernist, added elements of iron to many of the gold-covered statues.

The Parisians came to love the extravagant structure. Until the First World War, the building glittered with majestic balls, and provided the perfect setting for romantic love affairs conducted during intermissions and flirtations between adjoining boxes.

PLATE 56

PONT NATIONAL

The Pont National is officially classified as the twenty-ninth Parisian bridge out of a total of thirty-seven.

Like the Opéra, the bridge was part of the plan for urban renewal envisaged by Napoléon III and directed by Baron Haussmann, who together completely transformed the face of Paris during the Second Empire. Originally known as Pont Napoléon III, the bridge was renamed Pont National in 1870 following France's defeat by the Prussians.

The Pont National was built in 1852–3, designed by the engineers Couche and Petit to provide a route for the Petite Ceinture railway, the line that used to run around the periphery of the city and is now disused. In 1936 the bridge was doubled in width by the construction of a matching structure built in reinforced concrete. It was completed in July 1944, and took the

width of the Pont National to 34 meters, linking the Boulevard Poniatowski on the Right Bank to the Boulevard Masséna on the Left Bank.

These boulevards, which were named after Napoleon I's marshals, divide Paris from the surrounding suburbs. They were built over the former site of the city walls. Still under construction in 1900, the Boulevards des Maréchaux were finally completed in 1920.

PLATE 57

A PARISIAN CUISINE

A Parisian kitchen, lit only by candlelight, was organized around the most important element—a coal-fired stove.

At the beginning of the last century, the average Parisian diet became considerably richer and more varied, as well as healthier, primarily because of improvements in food preservation techniques.

Here we see a man working at the stove, perhaps in a restaurant. The first Paris restaurant was opened in 1765 by a café proprietor who decided to imitate the aristocracy's fashionable multicourse dining style. After the French Revolution, restaurants became common, the fleeing nobility having left behind many out-of-work domestic employees who thus found a market for their skills.

As opposed to at the *auberges* or inns, customers ate at individual tables and chose their meal. Some cooks made huge fortunes, such as Auguste Escoffier, "the king of the kitchen and cook to the kings," the "grammarian" of French cooking who founded a school that still welcomes students today at the Ritz in

Place Vendôme. Escoffier invented such culinary classics as Pêche Melba and Crêpes Suzette, and became head chef at the Carlton in London before joining César Ritz in Paris.

Marcel Proust often dined at the Ritz, and sometimes invited his friends to join him there. Opened in 1898, the establishment was an instant success. On opening day the celebrated society host Boni de Castellane was present, as well as a "mass of Rothschilds and Grand Dukes from Russia," as one newspaper put it. Every time a famous customer arrived, the majordomo would murmur, "I have saved the best table for Monsieur."

PLATE 58

PLACE DE LA CONCORDE

Only a century before Menpes captured it in this painting, the Place de la Concorde
was the gruesome scene of countless executions.

Over 1,100 people perished under the blade of the guillotine during the French Revolution. Marie Antoinette, preceded by her husband, Louis XVI, was beheaded in the Place de la Concorde on January 21, 1793. It was at the end of this horrific bloodbath, known as "The Terror," that the government decided to rename the square Place de la Concorde, *concorde* in French meaning "harmony."

The Place de la Concorde is the second largest square in France, after the Place des Quinquonces in Bordeaux. At its four corners are statues and fountains celebrating river and maritime navigation. The square's current incarnation began under Louis XV in 1748 as a dignified setting for an equestrian statue of the king, designed by Ange-Jacques Gabriel, the king's architect. In 1831 the viceroy of Egypt gave the square its inimitable cachet by placing there the Luxor obelisk, whcih still stands proudly at its center today.

By 1900 the Place de la Concorde, in complete contrast to its role during the Revolutionary period, had become a distinguished and decorous rendezvous for fashionable society. On one side of the square were the Tuileries Gardens, and on the other the palatial Hôtel Crillon with its luxurious tearoom. Farther down, the Rue Royale leads to the Place de la Madeleine, which can be seen to the left of the fountain in the background of the painting. This is home to one of Paris's finest restaurants, Maxim's.

PLATE 50

HÔTEL DES INVALIDES EN FÊTE

Another day, another celebration at the Invalides.

The golden dome of the Invalides shines in the sun, rising behind the marquees as the colorful crowd presses around the *tombola gratuite*, or free lottery, carefully keeping their umbrellas raised as protection from the sun. White skin, not suntans, was the fashion in those days.

The name Invalides, meaning "invalid" or "disabled," comes from the original purpose of the building, which was constructed in 1670 to shelter soldiers too disabled or elderly to continue to serve in the army. Four thousand inmates lived a monastic existence here, making rugs, repairing shoes, and sewing uniforms. A hospital, which is still in use today, was also part of the structure.

In 1706 the Église du Dôme, a masterpiece of classical French architecture, was erected. The tip of the dome, at 331 feet, was the highest point in Paris. Under Napoléon I, the Invalides became synonymous with the celebration of military victories, being the place where the Legion of Honor was awarded.

In 1840, during a nationwide funeral service, the emperor's ashes were repatriated from the Île Sainte-Hélène, where Napoléon had died a prisoner in 1821. By 1900, with the Second Empire crumbling before the Prussians, and under the governance of the less-than-popular Third Republic, the Parisian crowd was no doubt delighted to pay homage to that great French hero.

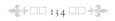

PLATE 60

BREAD SHOP NEAR CENTRAL MARKET

Menpes was charmed by the narrow streets surrounding Les Halles.

Here is a small boy playing with a balloon in front of a bakery window with its display of cakes and baguettes. Is he old enough to be at school yet, or is he still in the care of his mama or nursemaid? During the Third Republic, in 1882, school attendance became mandatory for children between the ages of six and twelve, boys and girls being educated separately in different establishments.

At the age of twelve, all children had to pass the *certificate d'études*, a compulsory examination. Some would go on to *collège*, or secondary school; others would be apprenticed to a trade or work for their parents. Children often wore the traditional *tablier* we see in the painting, a garment that buttoned up the back and protected their clothing. Most also wore the traditional wooden shoes called sabots, though this little boy, who is probably from a relatively well-off family, appears to be wearing galoshes.

The *instituteur*, or primary schoolteacher, was a symbol of the Republic and an important cultural figure. They were often called the *hussards noirs de la République*, "the black hussars of the Republic," because of their black coats and blackboards, the tools of their trade in spreading the Republican ideals of secularism, tolerance, reason, and enlightenment.

13e Année. — N°. 103   10 centimes.   16 novembre 1901.

LE

Petit Français illustré

JOURNAL DES ÉCOLIERS ET DES ÉCOLIÈRES

FRANCE : UN AN, 6 FRANCS (du 1er do chaque mois) | Librairie Armand Colin Paris, 5, rue de Mézières. | UNION POSTALE : UN AN, 7 FRANCS (Paraît chaque Samedi)

Une tâche difficile.

PLATE 61

A CORNER AT THE RUE DE SEINE

Today the neighborhood around the church of Saint-Germain-des-Prés
is *trés chic*—but this was by no means the case during the belle epoque.

In central Paris of the 1900s, only the Eighth Arrondissement on the Right Bank of the Seine was considered to be a "good" district, and it was here that the fashionable few were accustomed to meeting. The Rue de Seine, across the river on the Left Bank, was frequented by the masses, but was renowned for its excellent market produce, which explains why the market is so busy.

Originally the Rue de Seine was just a path, called the Pre aux Clercs, but in 1812 much of it was rebuilt. The delightful ensemble of ironwork, gables, windows, and staircases reflects a time when domestic architecture was meticulous in its decorative details. The facade of Number 57 is particularly fine, being decorated with sculpted masks and rebates, wrought-iron balconies, and a superb pediment.

Times changed again, however, and during the 1930s and 1940s the area began to rise in status, assisted by an influx of artists and intellectuals. These included the zazous (named after the song "Zaz Zuh Zaz" by American jazz musician Cab Calloway), rebels such as the writer and poet Boris Vian, the actress Juliette Greco, and the philosophers Jean-Paul Sartre and Simone de Beauvoir, all of whom chose Saint-Germain on the Left Bank as their favorite district, deliberately avoiding the Eighth Arrondissement. They danced to jazz in the café cellars until the small hours of the morning and conducted their endless discussions on Existentialism at the Café de Flore, not far from where Menpes painted this down-to-earth market scene.

PLATE 62

GOSSIPS

A hundred years on we can only guess what these gossips are talking about.

Interestingly the painter has chosen men, rather than women, to illustrate the title—old men sitting on benches in a park such as can still be seen in the village cafés of the south of France.

One of them is dressed as an Auvergnat, a man from the Auvergne, with a large black hat and blue coat. In the 1890s and 1900s Auvergnats opened many cafés in Paris, and even today they still own 40 percent of Parisian establishments. Many Auvergnats also played the *cornemuse landaise*, or bagpipes, for the popular *bals-musettes*, a style of music particular to the Auvergnat communities of the Fifth, Eleventh, and Twelfth Arrondisements.

Clearly our Auvergnat knows some fascinating stories, as the other two men, wearing *canotiers*, or boaters, lean forward to listen to him, while the woman, perhaps his wife or daughter, gives the child a snack.

Perhaps these gossips are talking about the Dreyfus Affair, or the Panama Scandal. Or about other current events of the time like improvements in the lives of Parisians since the working day had been officially shortened to 10½ hours a day. Or about Marie Curie, the first woman appointed to teach at the Sorbonne University at a time when women did not have the right to vote Or maybe about Louis Blériot, who, on July 25, 1909, became the first person to cross the English Channel in an airplane.

But perhaps they are just talking about a newly opened café.

PLATE 63

THE TROCADÉRO PALACE

It was on the esplanade of the Trocadéro, with the Eiffel Tower
behind him, that Adolf Hitler posed for photographers in 1940.

It is possible that Hitler chose the monument not only for its sweeping views, but also for its architectural style and statues, which bear some resemblances to Fascist architecture.

The square we see depicted here bears little resemblance to the Trocadéro as it was during the war, and as it still stands today. Menpes's painting shows the original building, which was built in the luminous and rounded Baroque style. Like so many other buildings of that period, including the Eiffel Tower and the Grand and Petit Palais, the Palace of Trocadéro was constructed for a World Exposition, this one in 1878. Its design was inspired by the Moorish style, and its name commemorates the taking of the fort of Cádiz in Spain in 1823, part of the French attempt to reestablish the Spanish monarchy. Though they are not shown in the painting, the palace was framed by two tall towers, inspired by the architecture of Seville and expressing love of music, the festive spirit, and joy.

The building in the painting was pulled down two years before the beginning of World War II, and replaced by the Palais de Chaillot, built for the 1937 Exposition, the last colonial exhibition to be held in Paris. At the time, France had the second largest colonial empire in the world, including large parts of Africa. The vast cupola with its arcades was replaced with an esplanade, baptized the Place des Droits de l'Homme, or "Human Rights Square." Today, the Marine Museum and the Museum of Man are housed here.

PLATE 64

POND AT THE TUILERIES

Menpes has captured a charming informal group of children,
gathered at the edge of the pond in the Tuileries Garden.

Why are these children leaning over the stone edge of the fountain? Are they feeding ducks with crusts of stale bread or watching the goldfish swarm to their offerings of bread crumbs, or are they sailing little homemade wooden boats? Model boats are a feature of the ponds in Parisian parks today just as they were a hundred years ago, though these children are clearly not of a class that would have had the elaborate yachts and motorboats seen in the Luxembourg Gardens or on the lake at the Bois de Boulogne, which often hosted races of scale models of real boats.

Menpes's genre scene successfully conveys the joy that animates this sunny afternoon. In all likelihood he painted these children on a Thursday, because in France during 1909, Thursday was a half-day for schoolchildren, whereas now Wednesday is a half-day. Then, as now, French children attend school on Saturday morning to compensate for their midweek break.

In the center of the group is a small girl, perhaps being looked after by her brother in the purple shirt and distinctive beret; they are surrounded by a crowd of young boys, while a couple of adolescents in their peaked caps look on. In a charming detail, the young child to the far left has been captured by the painter with his legs in the air, intent upon the scene unfolding before him.

PARIS. — Jardin des Tuileries.

PLATE 65

THE SEINE AT SUNSET

This is one of Menpes's most poetically rendered riverscapes of the Seine, that eminently paintable river.

A romantically pink sunset shading into violet, the blue-green water, and the sandy, wild banks of the Seine, all painted in liquid washes with the background bridge—probably the Pont National—only vaguely recognizable. We could almost be looking at a painting by James McNeill Whistler, Menpes's longtime teacher and friend, whose atmospheric river "nocturnes" were much admired by the star pupil, who called Whistler "my master."

Mortimer Menpes met Whistler in the early 1880s, by which time American-born Whistler had already spent three years in Paris working alongside innovative French painters including Gustave Courbet, Henri Fantin-Latour, and Alphonse Legros. During the 1860s and 1870s Whistler developed his trademark style, which he often called nocturnes because they were painted in the evening or early morning when details of a scene were reduced to impressions and flat washes of color. He deliberately used the musical term *nocturne* to suggest the fleeting, sensory nature of his technique.

In a famous 1885 London lecture, Whistler explained his love of painting riverscapes, telling how he preferred to paint "when the evening mist clothes the riverside with poetry, as with a veil, and the poor buildings lose themselves in the dim sky, and the tall chimneys become campanile." In this painting of the Seine, as in several of the other river scenes, we see Menpes modeling his style on that of Whistler, concentrating on areas of flat color, on broad shapes rather than detail, on emotion as much as fact.

The two painters became very close, Whistler being the godfather of Menpes's daughter Dorothy, who wrote the text of the 1909 *Paris*, and whose middle name was Whistler. In 1904 Menpes wrote an illustrated account of his lifelong friendship with Whistler entitled *Whistler as I Knew Him*.

PLATE 66

FACTORIES ON THE SEINE

As France's Industrial Revolution gathered pace, workers in these riverside factories began to organize.

The material conditions of Paris's working class improved enormously during the last quarter of the nineteenth century and the first decade of the twentieth. The increase in real wages that had begun in the 1870s continued to 1914, although consumer prices rose rapidly after 1900, which effectively canceled earlier gains. Working conditions continued to be oppressive, however, and it was often in the largest factories of the most mechanized industries that workers experienced the worst conditions. A ten-and-a-half-hour day was the norm, and anything less than a six-day week was unheard of. Most workers could count on at least a month and a half of unemployment every year, being laid off at short notice when demand dipped.

To combat such conditions, French trade union membership jumped from an insignificant 139,000 in 1890 to slightly over a million in 1913, and from this strengthened position workers became more willing to engage in strike activity. In 1890 the first national May Day strikes took place, demanding an eight-hour day. These demonstrations of new working-class militancy were often marked by violent confrontations, yet workers did make gains, winning concessions in more than a quarter of the organized strikes in the period.

By 1884 unions had acquired legal status, and, thanks to their efforts, working and living conditions began to improve. In 1895 this activity led to the creation of a national organization of trade unions, the Confédération Générale du Travail.

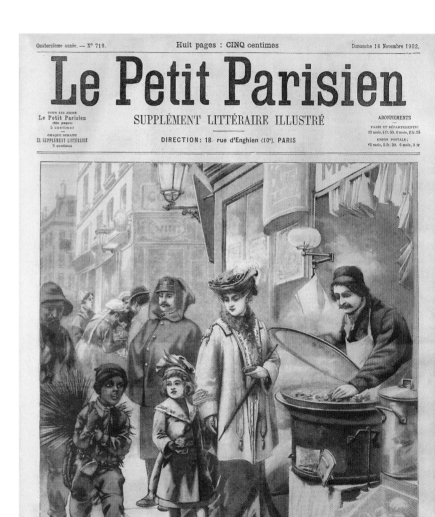

LES HIRONDELLES D'HIVER

LES GRÈVES DANS LE NORD

PLATE 67

BATHING-HOUSE (SAMARITAINE)

The floating bathhouses of the Samaritaine were as important to the city's social life as a Turkish hammam is to this day.

What a pleasure it must have been to bathe onboard ship, watching the *péniches* and ducks floating by just outside. The huge bathhouse depicted in this painting was built on a boat anchored next to the Pont Neuf in front of La Samaritaine, Paris's famous department store—the building can be seen just above the top of the boat. Palm trees were planted along the riverfront so that customers could enjoy an exotic ambience without having to leave their own city.

Unfortunately, when the Seine flooded in 1918, the boat capsized despite its strong anchor. The Samaritaine, however, continued to go from strength to strength, as did Paris's other *grands magasins* such as Le Bon Marché, the Galeries Lafayette, and the Printemps, which all still exist today.

Foreigners visiting Paris in 1909 would have been amazed to discover that luxury products had apparently become accessible to all. The number of products on offer made the stores a *bonheur des dames*—a paradise for women, as the French novelist Émile Zola described it in his 1883 novel based on life inside a Paris department store.

PLATE 68

FÊTE NEAR HÔTEL DES INVALIDES

This merry-go-round would have been as much of a tourist
attraction in 1909 as the enormous Ferris wheel is today.

The attractions on offer at the Invalides were quite remarkable for the period. During the Expositions Universelles, of which Paris hosted no fewer than six between 1855 and 1937, elaborate temporary buildings and attractions extended from the Champ de Mars under the Eiffel Tower to the Place des Invalides.

In her memoirs, Pauline de Broglie, sister of Nobel physics laureate Louis de Broglie and the leisured wife of a wealthy count, remembers the 1900 Exposition and tells of her admiration for a replica of the Rue d'Alger that included live camels, authentic Bedouins from the North African desert, and souks selling oriental carpets.

There was also an imitation Trans-Siberian, the railway linking Moscow with Vladivostok, a forty-five-minute simulated train ride with a moving panorama. A Swiss village, complete with cows and snow-covered mountains, generated more trepidation than any desire to scale them.

Even when these attractions had been demolished, Pauline de Broglie had many other amusements at her disposal. At the Boulevard des Capucines, her father would secretly take her to stand in line with the ordinary Parisians, where for one franc she could sit in a long, narrow room and watch films by the Lumière brothers. Never having been allowed to go to the circus, she found herself for the first time at the movies.

PLATE 69

MARCHÉ DE NEUILLY

Village people and weekend visitors gather around the stalls at Neuilly market.

The sleepy suburb of Neuilly-sur-Seine has always been a quiet place, but around the time Menpes made this painting, the town made history by being the location for the first public European flight of an airplane. On October 23, 1906, the Franco-Brazilian aviator Alberto Santos Dumont flew his *Oiseau de Proie* (*Bird of Prey*) at the town's bagatelle ground, which officially became the first autonomous flight of an aircraft flown with the exclusive use of an onboard propellant.

In addition to aeronautics, Neuilly was famous for horse racing. The Prix de Diane was held at nearby Chantilly, while the Jockey Club event at Longchamp was the favorite venue for the ultrachic to enjoy the racing atmosphere. It was the ideal place for the major fashion designers of the period, such as La Maison Redfern or Jacques Doucet, to showcase their latest creations.

But Neuilly was not a vacation spot. People came only for a weekend stay, spending their long vacations in Dieppe, in Normandy, or in Biarritz, on the southwestern coast of France.

72. SPORTS — Aviation - L'Aéroplane de M. Santos-Dumont couvrant 225 mètres et gagnant le prix Archdéacon

PLATE 70

BOOTH AT THE NEUILLY FÊTE

The festivities are about to begin in Neuilly, the town that gave its name to the famous Fête à Neu-Neu.

Here in the early morning the stands are being prepared to welcome crowds attracted to the excitement of the fete. Later in the day there will be games of chance and skill, including contests of strength, such as wrestling and tug-of-war, and stands exhibiting curiosities such as the bearded woman or the two-headed man. There will also be a plethora of games for children, such as the famous French game Colin Maillard, or blindman's buff.

Neuilly Fête had always had something a little risqué about it, which gave the usually constrained middle classes an opportunity to let their hair down. Thus the fete makes an appearance in Chapter 26 of Anatole France's 1894 novel *Le Lys Rouge* (*The Red Lily*), where a portrait of the protagonist Clara, made at the Neuilly Fête, makes an embarrassing reappearance. In the 1920s the belletrist Renée Dunan wrote to his lover,

Dora Adelphi, hoping that her Greek holiday was as exciting as the Neuilly Fête with its "bric-à-brac traders, pastries smelling of oil and saffron, sellers of resinous wines, olives in brine, fried tomatoes and fish grilled in cumin, fat philosophers, and laughing courtesans smelling of jasmine."

Fête de Neuilly. — La Loge de la Goulue

119

ND Phot

PLATE 71

A FISH STALL AT NEUILLY

Menpes was clearly charmed by the tranquillity of Neuilly, a quality the district retains to this day.

After tasting the pleasures of Charenton and its fairs, the world of workers and factories, Menpes focuses here on another market scene, this time showing us customers at a suburban fish market. Neuilly is located along one of the loops of the Seine, so doubtless much of the fish was fresh from the river, though there was always plenty of fish from farther afield. The specialty fish merchants from Brittany and Normandy would have met the early trains with their fresh catches, which meant that the discerning Neuilly housewife could have bought fresh lobster, sole, and many kinds of oyster.

Once spring arrived, it was considered quite the thing to leave Paris for the day and go to the country for one's health. People felt the need to breathe fresh air, as the widespread use of coal in the city's fireplaces made for poor air quality in the city. The grandes dames visiting Neuilly covered their hats with veils tied under their chin to protect themselves from the dust, while the men brought out their boaters.

Marchande de Poissons

Marchande de poissons

PLATE 72

WASH-HOUSE NEAR PONT NEUF

Bathing along the banks of the Seine was a common practice in 1909.

Today we can only dream of what once was, although Jacques Chirac, former president of the French Republic, once promised that by 1992 Parisians would be bathing in the Seine once more— a promise that, needless to say, he failed to keep. Back in 1909, washing in the river was common. A typical Parisian character of the time was the riverside barber, who plied his trade not in a shop but out in the open air under the bridges of the Seine. Customers could sit and watch the boats glide past as their hair was being cut or their beard shaved. This service was, of course, provided for men only.

If you were desirous of more privacy, you could attend one of the closed bathing establishments, such as the one represented in Menpes's painting. Inspired by the bathhouse boat anchored near the Pont Neuf, these establishments were also located in the very center of Paris. Although such public bathing facilities no

longer exist, some *bain-douches*, or "bath-shower" establishments, continued to operate for many years, mainly owing to the absence of private bathrooms in old apartments and poorer neighborhoods. From the 1980s onward these were refurbished, often as fashionable nightclubs.

PLATE 73

A FLOWER STALL

A woman sells large flower bouquets and potted plants on the banks of the Seine.

Today the Marché aux Fleurs, along the Seine on the Île de la Cité, still sells every kind of plant and flower imaginable, from the ordinary to the exotic.

Flowers are a quintessential part of the romance of Paris, known all over the world for being a city for lovers. Many Romantic poets and artists have lived and worked in the city, leaving their indelible mark on French culture—Frédéric Chopin, Franz Liszt, Eugène Delacroix, Ivan Turgenev, George Sand, and Alfred de Musset, among many others.

What could feel more romantic than murmuring, as you purchased one of these bouquets, a verse by Alfred de Musset from his *"A Une Fleur"* ("To a Flower") —

"What do you want from me, little flower,
Pleasant and charming remembrance.
Do you have a message for me?
Your fragrance is a language …
Say nothing, just let me dream."

Marchande de fleurs

PLATE 71

THE TUILERIES GARDENS

Although Menpes entitled this painting The Tuileries Gardens,
it actually depicts the usually bustling Jardin du Luxembourg.

A favorite spot for Parisians, the Jardin du Luxembourg has always been a gathering point for students from the surrounding universities and, of course, for children. A favorite pastime both then and now was sailing model ships in the large round fountain in the middle of the garden, just in front of the Palais du Luxembourg, where the French Senate holds session.

Created in 1612 by Maria de Médici, mother of Louis XIII, the Jardin du Luxembourg is a typically French garden with marble vases and balustrades, lavish statuary, square lawns, and fountains. From the angle depicted in Menpes's painting, the Pantheon, built on the Montagne Sainte-Geneviève, is visible across the garden.

The English tourist of 1909 would probably have been intrigued by the way the French raised their children, playing with them as much as they could, sharing biscuits and bottles of milk in the middle of the grass, playing hide-and-seek between the chestnut trees, and not caring too much if they dirtied dresses of silk and dainty lace frills, as the children of the rich mixed with their hatless friends in tattered clothing. Children would have gathered around to watch the antics of Guignol, the famous star of the traditional puppet show, full of drama and slapstick humor. For adults who wanted to play, tennis courts were provided within the garden.

PLATE 75

A CAKE STALL

What mouthwatering dessert shall we enjoy tonight?
Perhaps a deliciously sweet and moist *quatre-quarts*—the French version of pound cake.

Or perhaps lemon tart with a meringue topping. Or croissants, invented during the invasion of Vienna by the Turks in 1683, inspired by the Islamic half-moon.

Traditional French cakes have a long and rich history, many of them based on the traditions and foods of other cultures. From the humble *petite madeleine* to the mighty *croquembouche*, French pâtisserie is renowned as the best and most creative in the world, and though this humble cake stall would not have carried the range of the famous Parisian pâtissiers, such as Stohrer or Haupois, it would still have offered a tempting range of sweetmeats.

Babas au rhum were a great favorite, filled with rum-soaked raisins and brushed with rum and sugar syrup. This delectable cake was introduced to France by the Polish when Prince Stanislas Leczinski was forced to live in exile in Nancy. Parisian bakers took the *babas au rhum* to new heights with the *savarin*, a yeast cake dipped in kirsch-flavored sugar syrup. The name came from the famous gastronome Jean Anthelme Brillat-Savarin, who developed the recipe for the syrup.

At the humbler end of the cake spectrum was the *financier* or *friand*, a light tea cake that took its name from the rectangular gold-ingot-shaped mold in which it was baked, and *pain d'épices*, a traditional spice cake similar to gingerbread.

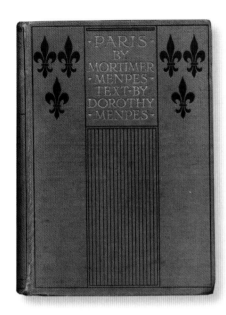

The trade edition of *Paris* (above), and the larger "edition-de-luxe," of which 500 signed copies were produced (below).

In all of A&C Black's color plate books it was the pictures that mattered. The words were a secondary consideration, as can be deduced from the lack of specific instructions to authors in the publisher's letters. The result is that texts vary widely both in length and style, from the heavily factual and historical to the anecdotal. Some are still worth reading today—those of Dorothy Menpes are not among them. Dorothy Whistler Menpes, the third child and second daughter of Mortimer Menpes, was only eighteen when *War Impressions*, the first in the series, appeared. Her role seems to have been as an amanuensis for her artist father, and this collaboration continued for a further six books. Adam Black became increasingly impatient with the inadequacies of some of her writing, rejecting her manuscript for *The Thames* and having *Venice* rewritten by different authors for later editions.

The complicated publishing history of *Paris* seems to be a consequence both of this dissatisfaction and of the publication of a rival book by Dent. First planned in 1903, publication of *Paris* in the 20 Shilling Series was eventually delayed until 1909. Dent's book appeared in 1904 as *Paris and Its Story* by Thomas Okey, with forty-four color illustrations by Katherine Kimball and O. F. M. Ward. A&C Black's correspondence first refers to *Paris* in a letter of December 1903, saying that a rival had been announced and they "must put our book in order at once and publish as soon as possible." In September 1904, however, Adam Black wrote to Mortimer Menpes: "Miss Dorothy promised the complete manuscript last Saturday, you promised it yesterday, but it has not yet come to hand. This means the book cannot be published at soonest before November and Dent announces his book as almost ready. One can only hope that Dent is not so far advanced as he makes out & that by making a big effort he can yet be forestalled."

Paris was first advertised in 1904, the prospectus stating that the first fifty copies of the large-paper edition would contain an original watercolor by Mortimer Menpes. By 1906 arrangements had been made to have a new text written, but these came to nothing, and eventually Dorothy's words were used when the book was first published in the 6 Shilling Series, using only twenty-four illustrations, in 1907.

In March 1908 A&C Black wrote to the publisher John Grant of Edinburgh: "In reply to your letter of today we have 3,000 each and over copies of 51 illustrations, which we are prepared to let you have for £100." A letter of September 23, 1908, says that A&C Black "are not prepared to accept your offer & we would remind you that the offer to sell the plates did not emanate from us. What we offered you for £100 cost us almost three times as much." And a final letter says: "In reply to your letter of yesterday if you will pay the £162 5s on Nov 1st we will put your order in hand at once and deliver by the end of May." The result was that *Paris* was published by Grant, but under the A&C Black imprint; it was printed by Oliver & Boyd in February 1909 in an edition of 3,050 copies, with a large paper limited and numbered edition of 500.

An American edition was issued by Charles L. Bowman and Company of New York in white cloth decorated in red and gilded; the British edition is in red cloth decorated in black and gilded. The cover design is by A. A. Turbayne, though his monogram is not present. No reprints are evident, and *Paris* can be regarded as among the scarcer of the 20 Shilling Series.

Paris represented Dorothy Menpes's last appearance as an author for A&C Black. In September 1909 she married Ivan Charles Flower, a stockbroker. They had a son and daughter. Dorothy died in 1973, meriting a brief obituary in the *Times*.

A New World of Color Printing

The cultured classes of the first decade of the twentieth century loved color, and great strides in printing and ink technology allowed them to have it, breaking free of the limitations of the monotone pages of their parents' generation with their woodcuts and steel engravings. Many of these developments came from Germany where, by the turn of the nineteenth century, there was a lucrative industry in color postcards, greeting cards, and books containing dozens of color illustrations.

The challenge and promise of color were quickly taken up in Britain, where presses—especially in London and Edinburgh—started to use the latest technology to print color plates for a range of reference books.

Until the early 1890s, anyone wanting to print a color image had to design the images in such a way that the different colors, each printed from its own plate, could easily be separated from each other. Many ways were developed to create subtlety in the use of color, including engraving fine detail into each color plate, using separate plates for different tones of the same color, and finishing each plate by hand after it had been printed. Even so, most color printing in 1900 was fairly crude, and it is clear—especially under the magnifying glass—that the drive for realistic color still had some way to go.

The best color printing in the 1900s, however, was stunning. In the period between 1900 and 1914, before war dried up ink and machinery supplies from Germany to the rest of the world, printing in color reached a peak that was not to be reached again until the 1960s.

It is important to remember that outdoor color photography as we know it, using color film to photograph places and people, was not invented until the 1930s. However, from about 1890 onward, several processes for making color photographs of inanimate objects in a studio setting were well advanced, and the printers of the period were amazingly inventive.

One of the greatest pioneers was a German emigrant, Carl Hentschel, who in the 1890s patented the Hentschel Colourtype Process and set up his company on London's Fleet Street. Hentschel developed a massive camera that used three color filters—red, green, and blue—to capture simultaneous images of any original flat color image. At the same time, developments such as the halftone screen, which allowed color gradation to be printed as an almost-imperceptible pattern of different-sized dots onto paper, were enabling photographed images to be transferred to paper, both in black and white and in the new three-color process.

It was now possible to photograph flat objects like paintings—or small groups of objects in a studio setting—in color. And it was possible to use those images, separated into their three component process

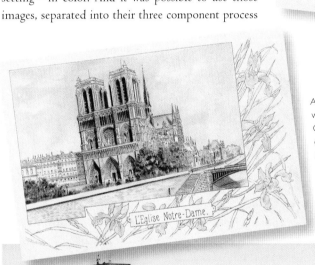

An 1893 poster by Jules Chéret, a lithographer whose shop became part of the Imprimerie Chaix and who was one of the first artists to draw straight onto the litho stone (above); Notre Dame, from an 1890s collection of watercolors entitled *Souvenir—Paris et ses Environs* (left); Place de la République from another souvenir guide produced by Établissements Papeghin for the 1900 Exposition (below).

colors, to print color images. It was impossible, however, to make color photographs of the wide outside world, of cities, mountains, and crowds of people. Yet once they had a taste of color postcards and color pictures in books, those who could afford to buy such relatively expensive luxuries wanted as much color as they could get.

The images in this book demonstrate the many ways in which the inventors, photographers, and publishers of the period strove to give their customers what they so craved—the real world on the printed page in full color.

THE HENTSCHEL THREE-COLOR PROCESS

In 1868, when he was four years old, Carl Hentschel moved to London from the Russian-Polish city of Lodz with his family. Like his father, he became an engraver, and by 1900 was an important figure in color printing and in London's social life. As well as being an active advocate of his innovative printing process, he was a founding member of several clubs, including the Playgoer's Club and, as a great friend of Jerome K. Jerome, was the model for Harris in Jerome's *Three Men in a Boat.*

Although not the inventor of the three-color halftone process—it had been developed by Frenchmen Louis du Hauron and Charles Cros and American Frederick Ives in the 1870s—Hentschel's company led the way in using the method on a commercial scale.

The process is well described in Burch's 1906 book *Colour Printing and Colour Printers*: "Once the principle is accepted that any combination of colours can be resolved into its primary elements, it remains only for the photographer to obtain three negatives which automatically dissect the original, making three distinct photographic records of the reds, yellows and blues which enter into the composition. The result is obtained by the use of transparent screens of coloured pigment or liquid, 'light filters' as they are technically termed, placed in front of the lens. These filters admit any two of the primary colours and absorb the other one. Three separate screens are employed,

each with the lines ruled at a different angle, and when the negative records of the colour analysis are obtained, the three photographs are converted into printing surfaces."

Among Hentschel's growing list of customers was Adam Black, the original "A" of A&C Black, who early on recognized the Colourtype process as the one that would give his publishing company a head start in the production of color books. In its time, it must have seemed magical that color plates could be produced to such a high standard and—at only four hours from photograph to finished printing plate—so quickly.

COLOR POSTCARDS

The first decade of the twentieth century was the high tide of the postcard craze, which used the new technologies of color printing and the newly introduced postcard postage rate to fill drawing rooms with pictures from all over the world. In 1899 the British Post Office gave in to popular pressure to allow postcards to have more than just the address written on the back, which allowed publishers to use all of the picture side to display their design. Other countries quickly followed suit.

Postcard publishers rapidly increased production to fill the demand for postcards, these cards being the one product line that constantly pushed color printing to the limits of what was achievable. Many color postcards were printed in Germany, or

Carl Hentschel (top) and the original "three men in a boat" (below)—Carl Hentschel, George Wingrave, and Jerome K. Jerome.

The chromographoscope (below), invented by Louis Ducos du Hauron in 1874, was a dual-purpose machine. It could be used as a camera or as an additive viewer.

Boulevard des Italiens, a postcard of c.1905.

by companies with German origins. None was more inventive, productive, and formative than the London-based company of Raphael Tuck and Sons. Raphael Tuch (his original name) moved to London with his wife and eleven children from Breslau in Prussia in 1865. He opened a small shop in Whitechapel, moving in 1870 to City Road, where he and his sons Adolph, Herman, and Gustave helped develop a range of photographs and scraps, much of it imported from Germany. In 1871 came the first Christmas card, and in 1876 the colored oleograph. The breakthrough year for the postcard was 1894, when Tuck produced a card with a vignette of Snowdon in North Wales.

In the first decades of the postcard's life, there were three ways of producing a color image. You either started with a real black-and-white photograph and added subtle layers of color to indicate water or a sunset, used traditional color engravers to create separated color designs from scratch, or used the new three-color process to photograph painted originals. It was this third option that allowed companies like Raphael Tuck and Sons to expand so rapidly, and they were quick to commission a number of excellent artists to create series of paintings specifically for reproduction as postcards.

PHOTOCHROMES

Of all the methods for colorizing photographic images before outdoor color photography, the photochrome process was probably the most successful. The brilliantly colored prints displayed at the 1889 Paris Exposition by the Swiss company Orell Füssli and Co. won a gold medal, and their realism thrilled those who saw them. Only three companies—Füssli's own Photoglob in Switzerland, Photochrom in Britain, and the Detroit Printing Company in the United States—were ever licensed to use the "secret" technique, which by 1910 had resulted in more than 13,000 color images of every corner of Europe and the landmarks of North America, India, and North Africa.

Each photochrome required intensive labor, an artistic eye, and, ideally, an accurate record of what colors were actually present in the scene portrayed. A

film negative was used as the basis for creating a series of lithographic plates—flat pieces of stone quarried in Bavaria and coated with asphaltum, one stone for each color. The negative had to be retouched by hand for each color, sometimes with fourteen different colors being used, then the stone exposed to sunlight for several hours before it was developed with turpentine. Each stone was hand-finished with the additional development of chosen areas using fine pumice powder before being etched in acid to reveal the image ready for printing. Special semitransparent inks were then used to transfer the image from the stones onto smooth paper, and finally each printed image was varnished to bring out its depth and richness.

The British Photochrom Company, with offices in London and Tunbridge Wells, published a series of twenty photochrome images of Paris, available to the public as prints for framing and as postcards. These and more than 5,000 other photochromes can be seen online at www.ushistoricalarchive.com/photochroms/index.html.

L'Arc de Triomphe and the Tomb of the Unknown Soldier, from a souvenir viewbook published in 1900 by Établissements Papeghin (above); two photochromes of the 1900 Exposition (below).

THE TURBAYNE BINDINGS

When they launched the 20 Shilling Series of colored books in 1903, A&C Black knew full well that, in order to sell books at such a high price, the look of the book from the outside was just as important as the innovative color used on the inside.

American-born Albert Angus Turbayne moved to London in the early 1890s and established a close association with the pioneering bindery at the Carlton Studio. By 1903 his William Morris—inspired designs were considered to be the pinnacle of the bookbinder's art. His forte was the combination of exuberant blocking, often in three or four colors, and beautifully executed lettering, but one of the bindery's greatest skills was in creating designs that exactly matched the subject of the book. Albert Turbayne always did extensive research into his subject, consulting libraries and illustrated books to find precisely the right elements with which to illustrate each of the Black books.

The design details of the present series of Memories of Times Past books pay homage to the skills of the Turbayne Bindery. The designs in the side panels of the cover are derived from the original covers of the A&C Black books, and the decorative elements within the book echo these designs, thus maintaining the theme and feel that Turbayne strove to achieve.

SOURCES, NOTES, AND CAPTIONS

The images used to complement the paintings come from a wide variety of sources, including books, postcards, museums, and libraries. They include photochromes, ephemera, advertisements, and maps of the period. The photochromes, and more than 5,000 others, can be seen online at www.ushistoricalarchive.com/photochroms/index.html. The large colored numbers refer to the plate numbers.

1 Middle: newspaper kiosk, from *Things Seen in Paris*, Clive Holland, Seeley Service, 1930. Left: advertisement for absinthe from *Le Rire*, 1904. Right: cover of *Le Petit Journal*, September 3, 1911.

2 Right: Cover of *Petit Parisien*, January 11, 1903. Left: La Bourse, from *Vues de Paris*.

3 Top left: Notre Dame, from *Paris* by Établissements Papeghin, *c.* 1901. Top right: a 1906 postcard of Notre Dame. Below: a map of the First Arrondissement from *Paris-Atlas*, Librairie Larousse, *c.* 1910.

4 Top left: Jardin des Tuileries from *Paris-Atlas*. Middle: double-page spread map of the First Arrondissement from *Plan de Paris par Arrondissement* by L. Guilmin, *c.* 1906.

5 Top left: Pont du Carrousel, painted by Lucien Gautier, from *The Spirit of Paris* by Frankfort Sommerville, A&C Black, 1913. Bottom: Panorama sur La Seine vers la Tour Eiffel, from *Paris*, by Établissements Papeghin.

6 Top left: postcard "offerte par le Grand Bazar de l'Hôtel de Ville," *c.* 1906. Middle: La Place de l'Hôtel de Ville, from *Paris-Atlas*. Below: Hôtel de Ville detail, from a map in *Baedeker's Guide*.

7 Middle left: Rue Lafayette, detail of an 1891 painting by Edvard Munch. Middle: Jean Jaurès, *c.* 1908. Bottom right: Jean Jaurès' last public meeting in 1913, from a contemporary postcard.

8 Main image: Map of the Twelfth Arrondissement showing the Pont de Tolbiac, from *Paris-Atlas*. Right: a modern image of the Bibliotheque Nationale de France, Flickr Creative Commons.

9 Top left: Hôtel de Ville, from *Paris-Atlas*. Main picture: L'Hôtel de Ville Eiffel, from *Paris*, by Établissements Papeghin.

10 Bottom left: Le Grand Palais, from *The Colour of Paris*, edited by M. Lucien Descaves and illustrated by Yoshio Markino, Chatto and Windus, 1914. Top right: the Fourth Arrondissement, from *Paris-Atlas*. Bottom right: La Rue des Grands Augustins from *Paris, A Sketch Book*, by Eug Bejot, A&C Black, 1912.

11 Left: La Samaritaine advertisement for toys and gifts from *Toys, Dolls, Games: Paris 1903–14*, Denys Ingram, 1981. Middle: a modern image of the Samaritaine stairway, Flickr Creative Commons. Right: La Parisienne, by an unknown artist, from *The Spirit of Paris* by Frankfort Sommerville, A&C Black, 1913.

12 Top left: *Versailles and Les Trianons* guidebook, printed by L. Pavillet, Rue Satory, Versailles, *c.* 1905. Middle: spread from *Souvenir: Paris et ses Environs*, Nouvelle Librairie de la Jeunesse, *c.* 1908. Bottom: 30 centime ticket for *bains froids* (left) and ticket for *chaises: grandes eaux et fêtes de nuit* (right).

13 Left: La Tour St. Jacques from *Paris Photochroms*. Middle: François Couperin. Right: Eglise St. Gervais, from *Paris-Atlas*.

14 Top: Notre Dame, book boxes on the *quais*, from *Things to See in Paris*. Top right: Les bouquinistes, from *Paris Pittoresque*, Vol. II by K.F. Éditeurs (the cover has a sticker giving a price of 1 franc 10c). Bottom left: cover of *Things Seen in Paris*. Middle left: cover of *The Spirit of Paris*. Bottom right: bookstalls on the Seine embankment, by Yoshio Markino, from *The Colour of Paris*.

15 Top: Charles Baudelaire. Bottom right: Rue de Seine, Sixth Arrondissement, from *Paris-Atlas*. Bottom left: Rue de Seine, viewed from the window of the Hôtel l'Ancienne Commedie, a 1904 painting by T. F. Šimon.

16 Below: Pont des Arts et l'Institute de France, from *Paris-Atlas*. Top right: poster for the film "Pont des Arts."

17 Top left: École des Beaux Arts, from *Paris-Atlas*. Right: Facade et Dome, Institut Francais, from *Paris-Atlas*. Below left: Pont du Carrousel, *c.* 1890, artist unknown, Wikimedia.

18 Left: devil and pelican gargoyle, Notre Dame, from *Paris-Atlas*. Right: Notre Dame, illustration by Hanslip Fletcher from *The Path to Paris*, Bodley Head, 1908.

19 Below left: a 1900s postcard of le Port Mazas and le Pont d'Austerlitz. Right: l'Ancien Muséum avec les Baleines, Le Jardin des Plantes, from *Paris Pittoresque*. Below right: front cover of Le Jardin des Plantes, from *Paris Pittoresque*.

20 Top left: flooded platforms at the Gare d'Orsay, from *Innondations de Paris*, 1910. Below left: 1904 postcard of the Quai d'Orsay. Right: 1900s postcard of La Grande Roue.

21 Bottom: "The Seine at Charenton, 1878," by Armand Guillaumin. Top right: Hôtel de Ville, Charenton-le-Pont, also known as le Pavillon Antoine de Navarre.

22 Left: 1906 postcard of le Canal St. Martin et la Colonne de Juillet. Right: modern photograph of the same scene, Flickr Creative Commons.

23 Main picture: Marchande des Quatre-Saisons, from *Scènes Parisiennes*.

24 Middle: La Soupe aux Halles, from *Paris Pittoresque*. Left: map showing Halles Centrales, First Arrondissement, from *Paris-Atlas*. Right: poster by Georges Rochegrosse for the opera *Louise*, written by Gustav Charpentier and performed at the Théatre National de l'Opéra Comique.

25 Middle: Chrysanthemum Fair, cover of *Petit Parisien*, November 20, 1910. Top left: Quai aux Fleurs, from *Paris Pittoresque*, Series IV.

26 Middle: Eugene Atget, photograph by Berenice Abbott, *c.* 1923. Bottom left: Eugene Atget, Organ Grinder, 1898. Right: Eugene Atget, The Cuviér Fountain at the Corner of Rue Linné, 1899.

27 Middle: elegant town costume by Louise Piret, Rue Richer, 1910, from *La Mode Illustrée*. Right: Les Petits Metiers de Paris: Une Marchande des Quatre-Saisons, from *La Belle Epoque*. Left: a 1910 postcard showing a *chapeau aigrette*—from the French for egret, whose head feathers were used for adorning women's hats.

28 Middle: an 1898 poster by Lucien Lefèvre for Absinthe Mugnier. Right: 1900s postcard of a female billsticker putting up a poster for Les Folies Bergère. Left: front cover of the first U.S. edition of *L'Assommoir* by Émile Zola.

29 Middle: a one-centime coin of 1912. Right: La Soupe des Pauvres, cover of *Le Petit Francais Illustré*, December 8, 1900. Below left: Les Pauvres, from *Le Petit Francais Illustré*, June 8, 1901.

30 Main picture: "Soleil Couchant a Ivry, 1873," by Armand Guillaumin.

31 Right: Charenton—Le Pont Embarcadère des Bateaux Parisiens, Wikimedia. Left: "The Seine at Charenton, 1907," by J. D. Fergusson.

32 Middle: map showing Charenton in the bottom right-hand corner, *Paris-Atlas*. Right: Dessin de Cheval, *La Baionette*, November 18, 1915. Left: "The Bridge of Charenton, 1898," by Edward Willis Redfield.

33 Left: 1910 postcard of Bois de Vincennes Vélodrome Municipale. Middle: 1897 poster by Léo Gausson for Lessive Figaro. Right: 1899 poster by Roedel 1899 for Linge Monopole.

34 Right: Kiosks in the Grand Boulevard, by Yoshio Markino, from *The Colour of Paris*. Right: walking suit in cyprus green wool, 1910, from *La Mode Illustrée*.

35 Right: glass and china repairer, from *Things Seen in Paris*. Left: les petits métiers de la rue marchands de journaux, from *La Belle Epoque*.

36 Top right: *ball coiffure* by Maison Heng, Rue Bergere, 1909, from *La Mode Illustrée*. Below left: Entrée du Palais de l'Elysée, from *Paris-Atlas*. Bottom right: Le 5 o'clock, from *The Spirit of Paris*.

37 Top right: Crue de la Seine—la statue de Zoave baignant dans l'eau, January 1910, from *La Belle Epoque*. Bottom right: Crue de la Seine—Pont d'Alma, January 28, 1910, from *Retour à Paris*. Right: The Pont d'Alma by Yoshio Markino, from *The Colour of Paris*.

38 Right: Quai aux Fleurs by Harry Morley, from *The Charm of Paris*. Top middle: "Rose," by The Engraving Company Ltd., from *Penrose's Pictorial Annual, 1913–14*. Left: an 1898 poster by René Péan.

39 Main picture: Halles Centrales et Eglise St. Eustache, from *Paris-Atlas*.

40 Below right: design by Ray Ordner from *La Baionette*, April 26, 1917. Top right: "Peaches," frontispiece from *Thompson's Gardeners Assistant*, Vol. 5, Gresham Publishing Co., 1902. Left: "Plums," from *Familiar Trees*, Vol. 1, Cassell and Co., 1906.

41 Bottom right/top left: 1900s postcard of Bois de Boulogne: Allée des Acacias. Bottom left: postcard of Neuilly sur Seine—Rue Jacques Dubud and Avenue de Neuilly. Top right: postcard of Neuilly sur Seine—Rue Montrosier.

42 Right: François Pilâtre de Rozier's balloon flight. Top right: "Jardin des Tuileries, 1912," by Pierre Bonnard. Below: In the Tuileries Gardens by Mortimer Menpes, *World's Children*, A&C Black, 1903.

43 Left: 1893 poster of Jane Avril at the Jardin de Paris, by Henri de Toulouse-Lautrec. Right: 1898 poster for the Moulin Rouge by Jules Chéret.

44 Top: portrait of Whistler by Mortimer Menpes, from *Whistler as I Knew Him*, A&C Black, 1904. Below: Pont des Arts and the Port St. Nicolas, from *Autrefois Paris Aujourd'hui*.

45 Left: Le marchand de lait, Montpelier, from *La Belle Epoque*. Below right: butter makers, from *The Book of the Home*, Vol. 3, Gresham, 1903.

46 Top left: Notre Dame, panorama from the tower, from *Things to See in Paris*. Below left: a 1910 postcard of Port de la Tournelle. Right: Rebuilding the Pont Tournelle, by Henry Rushbury, from *Paris*, by Sidney Dark, Macmillan, 1926.

47 Main picture: Le Palais du Louvre from *Paris*, Établissements Papeghin.

48 Left: Becassine, *c.* 1920. Right: Market Day, Brittany, by Mortimer Menpes, from *World's Children*.

49 Right: Poster for "Boudu Sauvé des Eaux," a film by Jean Renoir from the play by Réné Fauchois. Left: Vue de las Seine prise du Louvre, Pont des Arts, Pont Neuf, etc., from *Paris-Atlas*.

50 Right: La Nouvelle Gare de Lyon, *Petit Parisien*, March 16, 1902. Left: La Seine depuis le Pont de Bercy, *Autrefois Paris Aujourd'hui*.

51 Left: Armenonville in the Bois de Boulogne, one of the most famous of the fashionable restaurants, from *The Spirit of Paris*. Right: café chantant in the Champs Elysées, by Yoshio Markino, from *The Colour of Paris*.

52 Right: a 1910 postcard—Fête de Neuilly: American aviator. Left: Fête de Neuilly poster, June/July 1905.

53 Left: Façade Nord de l'hotel des Invalides, *Paris-Atlas*. Right: Un Jour de Congé (A Day Off), *Petit Francais Illustré*, June 8, 1901.

54 Right: Gare d'Orleans, Pont Solferino, by Yoshio Markino, from *The Colour of Paris*. Left: Pont de Solferino map, First Arrondisement, *Paris-Atlas*.

55 Right: Rue de la Paix at the Corner of the Place de l'Opéra, from *The Spirit of Paris*. Below left: L'Opéra, from *Paris* by Établissements Papeghin. Top: Le Grand Opéra, from *Souvenir: Paris et ses Environs*.

56 Top: Petite-Ceinture, Buttes Chaumont, Wikimedia. Below: Pont Nationale, *Paris-Atlas*.

57 Left: Au Pré Catelan, Bois de Boulogne, a high-class dining place in the Bois de Boulogne, from *The Spirit of Paris*. Right: illustration of a chef by Dudley Hardy, from *Homes of the Passing Show*, Savoy Press, 1900.

58 Main picture: Place de la Concorde, from *Paris* by Établissements Papeghin. Top right: Place de la Concorde, from *Vues de Paris: Heliochromes*.

59 Left: Le Dôme des Invalides, from *Souvenir: Paris et ses Environs*. Right: Le Dôme des Invalides, from *Paris* by Etablissements Papechin.

60 Left: École de Brazy en Morvan, 1900. Right: cover of *Petit Francais Illustré*, November 16, 1901.

61 Left: Monmartroise artistic type, from *The Spirit of Paris*. Right: Rue de Seine, by Henry Rushbury, from Sidney Dark's *Paris*, 1926.

62 Left: an 1892 poster for The Auvergne by Jules Chéret. Right: Bleriot's Flight, cover of *Petit Parisien*, August 8, 1909.

63 Main picture: La Palais de Trocadero Invalides, from *Paris* by Établissements Papeghin.

64 Below: Gardens of the Tuileries by Yoshio Markino, from *The Colour of Paris*. Top left: Jardin des Tuileries, from *Autrefois Paris Aujourd'hui*. Top right: Le Grand Bassin de Jardin des Tuileries, from *Paris-Atlas*.

65 Top: Menpes and Whistler, photograph from *Whistler as I Knew Him*. Bottom left: "Nocturne—Grey and Silver, The Thames, 1872," by Whistler. Middle: "Blue and Silver—Cremorne Lights, 1872," by Whistler. Bottom right: front cover of *Whistler as I Knew Him*.

66 Right: Les Hirondelles d'Hiver, cover of *Le Petit Parisien*, November 16, 1902. Left: Les Grèves dans le Nord, *Le Petit Parisien*, November 2, 1902.

67 Bottom: Les Bains de la Samaritaine et le Quai du Louvre, from *Paris-Atlas*. Top left: 1899 poster by Misti for Savon le Petit Chat.

68 Top left: detail from an 1899 poster by René Péan for the Boulevard de la Madeleine store Aux Trois Quartiers. Right: La Village Suisse a l'Exposition de 1900, from *l'Exposition de Paris, 1900*, Vol. 1. Below: Les Pavilions des Nations le Long de la Seine, from *l'Europe d'Autrefois*.

69 Left: design by d'Hérouard from *La Baionette*, December 16, 1915. Right: a 1906 postcard of Santos Dumont's record-breaking 225-meter flight.

70 Below left: At the Fair, by Mortimer Menpes, from *World's Children*. Below right: detail from an 1897 poster by Jules Cheret entitled *Redoute des Etudiants* (Students' Ball). Top right: a 1910 postcard of Fête de Neuilly—La Loge de la Goulue.

71 Top right: Marchande de Poissons (panier au bras), from *Paris Pittoresque*. Top: Marchande de Poissons (sur un eventaire), also from *Paris Pittoresque*. Below left: Plaice and Fillets, from *The Book of the Home*, Vol. 3.

72 Right: Anglers on the Seine, by Yoshio Markino, from *The Colour of Paris*. Middle: 1900s postcard of a Paris barber, Quai de Rouen. Below left: Washhouses on the Seine, by Henry Rushbury, from Sidney Dark's *Paris*, 1926.

73 Top right: Marchande de Fleurs from *Paris Pittoresque*. Below right: Paris in the Early Morning, from *The Spirit of Paris*. Left: Sweet peas, from *Penrose's Pictorial Annual, 1905 to 1906*.

74 Top right: Le Bassin du Luxembourg, from *Paris-Atlas*. Top left: Le Panthéon, from *Paris* by Établissements Papeghin. Bottom: Le Palais de Luxembourg, also from Papeghin's *Paris*.

75 Top left: blueberry friand. Below right: pain d'epices à l'orange. Below left: "What Shall I Eat?" from *Our Darlings*, John F. Shaw and Co., 1906.

BIBLIOGRAPHY

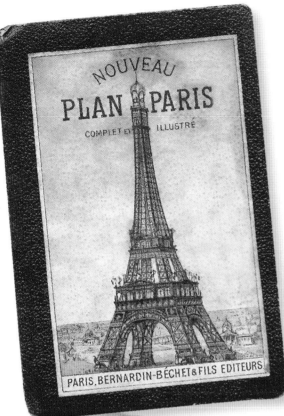

Age of Opulence: The Belle Epoque in the Paris Herald, 1890–1914, Hebe Dorsey, Harry N. Abrams, 1986.

Autrefois Paris Aujourd'hui, Gérard Chenuet, Reader's Digest, 2001.

Baedeker's Handbook to Paris, 1909.

The Charm of Paris, compiled by Alfred H. Hyatt and illustrated by Harry Morley, Chatto and Windus, 1920.

The Colour of Paris, edited by M. Lucien Descaves, Chatto and Windus, 1914.

The Complete Masters of the Poster, Stanley Appelbaum, Dover, 1990.

Cook's Guide to Paris, Thomas Cook & Son, 1910.

Exposition de Paris 1900, Volumes 1–3, Librairies Illustrée, 1900.

Femina, No. 94, 1904.

Guide Général de Paris: Répertoire des Rues, Raymon Denaës, Editions L'Indispensable, n.d.

Armand Guillaumin, Christopher Gray, Gray, 1972.

Homes of the Passing Show, The Savoy Press, 1900.

Inondations de Paris: Janvier 1910, R. Baudouin, 1910.

La Belle Epoque: Les Années 1900 par la Carte Postale, Serge Zeyons, Larousse, 1991.

L'Europe d'Autrefois, Aude Remy and Jean-Jacques Brisebarre, Reader's Digest, 2006.

Le Petit Journal Illustré, 1910–11.

Le Petit Français Illustré, 1901.

Nouveau Paris Monumental, Garnier Frères, n.d.

Nouveau Plan Paris, Bernardin-Béchet et Fils, n.d.

Paris, Sidney Dark, Macmillan, 1926.

Palais, Parc et Trianons de Versailles, A Cossé, n.d.

Paris, Établissements Papeghin, n.d.

Paris 1908: Plan du Métropolitain, n.d.

Paris: A Sketch Book, Eugène Bejot, A&C Black, 1912.

Paris-Atlas, Fernand Bournon, Librairie Larousse, n.d.

Paris et ses Environs, Nouvelle Librairie de la Jeunesse, 1906.

Paris 1900: The Art of the Poster, Hermann Schardt, Portland House, 1987.

Paris 1900–1914: The Miraculous Years, Nigel Gosling, Weidenfeld and Nicolson, 1978.

Portrait d'un Monde en Couleurs, Marc Walter and Sabine Arqué, Solar, 2007.

Retour à Paris, Parigramme, 2005.

Sandrine's Paris, Sandrine Voillet, BBC, 2007.

Souvenir Paris et ses Environs, L. Westhausser Dambuyant and Guignard, Nouvelle Librairie de la Jeunesse, n.d.

Things Seen in Paris, Clive Holland, Seeley, Service, 1945.

The Spirit of Paris, Frankfort Sommerville, A&C Black, 1913.

Toys, Dolls, Games: Paris 1903–1914, Denys Ingram, 1981.

Versailles: Souvenir, A. Bourdier, n.d.

Victorian and Edwardian Fashions from La Mode Illustrée, JoAnne Olian, Dover, 1998.

Vues de Paris, n.d.

Whistler as I Knew Him, Mortimer Menpes, A&C Black, 1904.

THE TIMES PAST ARCHIVE

The Memories of Times Past series would be inconceivable without the massive Times Past Archive, a treasury of books, magazines, atlases, postcards, and printed ephemera from the golden age of color printing between 1895 and 1915.

From the time several years ago when the project was first conceived, the collecting of material from all over the world has proceeded in earnest. As well as a complete set of the ninety-two A&C Black 20 Shilling color books, which are the inspiration for the series, the archive houses full sets of period *Baedeker* and *Murray's Guides*; almost every color-illustrated travel book from illustrious publishing houses like Dent, Jack, Cassell, Blackie, and Chatto & Windus; and a massive collection of reference works with color plates on subjects from railways and military uniforms to wildflowers and birds' eggs.

The archive also contains complete runs of all the important periodicals of the time that contained color illustrations, including the pioneering *Penrose's Pictorial Annual: An Illustrated Review of the Graphic Arts*; the first-ever British color magazine, *Colour*; ladies' magazines like *Ladies' Field* and the *Crown*; and more popular titles such as the *Connoisseur* and the *London Magazine*.

These years were vintage years for atlas publishing, and the Times Past Archive contains such gems as Keith Johnston's *Royal Atlas of Modern Geography*, *The Harmsworth Atlas*, Bartholomew's *Survey Atlas of England and Wales*, and *The Illustrated and Descriptive Atlas of the British Empire*.

Last but not least, the archive includes a wealth of smaller items—souvenirs, postcards, tickets, programs, catalogs, posters, and all the colorful ephemera with which the readers of the original 20 Shilling books would have been familiar.

THE TIMES PAST WEB SITE

The Web site to accompany this project can be found at www.memoriesoftimespast.com, where you will find further information about the birth and development of the project, together with the complete original texts of titles published to date. There is also an area where you can take part in discussions raised by readers of the books who want to take their interest further and share their memories and passions with others. The Web site will start small and elegant, as you would expect of an "Edwardian Web site," but it will gradually become what you and we together make it, a place for devotees of art and culture from a century ago to meet and be inspired.

Panorama des Huits Ponts de Paris, from *Paris*, a book of forty color plates produced in around 1903, by Établissements Papeghin.

Ligne de Charlebourg
Engrais de Javel
Manufacture
Courbevoie
Nanterre
Rond Point de Courbevoie
Bécon
Clichy
Courcelles
Villiers
Le Vallois-Perret
Les Batignolles
Monceaux
Neuilly
Puteaux
Sablonville
Les Ternes
Bagatelle
Fteresse du MontValérien
Ruel
Suresmes
Briqueterie
Fouilleuse
Hippodr. de Longchamp
Bois de Boulogne
La Muette
Passy
Chau Rothschild
Auteuil
Pte d'Auteuil
Bergerie
St Cloud
Garches
Boulogne
Grenelle
Point du Jour
Vaugirard
Parc de St Cloud
Lanterne
Ville d'Avray
Billancourt
Issy
Lycée
Malakoff
Bellevue
Bas Meudon
Sèvres
Vanves
Ft d'Issy
Montrouge
Pt Montrouge
Les Capucins
Le Val
Versailles
Meudon
Ft de Vanves
Ft de Montrouge
Bas Chaville
Chaville
Fleury
Clamart
Châtillon
La Croix d'Arcueil